IMPERFECT *Lives*
Perfect GRACE

IMPERFECT *Lives* *Perfect* GRACE

The Story of Leah and Tamar

DR. E.M. JOHNSON

ISBN: 979-8-88759-485-9 (Paperback)
ISBN: 979-8-88759-529-0 (Hardcover)
ISBN: 979-8-88759-486-6 (e-book)

Library of Congress Control Number: 0000000000

Printed by Jéan Benazir Press, in the United States of America

First printing edition 2023
Jéan Claude Publishers
P.O. Box 12415
Columbus, OH 43212

Unless otherwise noted all Bible quotations are from the World English Bible version of the Bible from biblegateway.com.

For the Leahs and Tamirs who walk among us. Your worst day is not your only day and your life will achieve the destiny and purpose that God has spoken. You are loved. You are beautiful. You bring light and hope to others.

For every person who serves as a voice for the silenced and an advocate for the abused.

CONTENTS

PREFACE

Leah and Tamar were two extraordinary women from the pages of scriptures whose experiences speak to the needs and struggles of contemporary life. Without realizing it, they became teachers for those who walked with them and those who followed later. There are lessons to be learned from their lives.

Leah, like many women, found herself in a less-than-perfect marriage. Based on a lie and deliberate deceit that was soon exposed, the marriage was troubled at best. Because of the shaky foundation, it was an uphill battle for her to gain trust and affection. The woman Jacob loved, the woman he wanted, was not Leah but her sister Rachel. Jacob was always honest about this fact, which made the marital deceit all the more painful. To say the Jacob-and-Leah union had a difficult start is an understatement. Many base their view of Leah on this one situation, this one act, and fail to view her as the total woman she became.

Leah was, nevertheless, a woman who loved her husband and family despite how it looked from the outside.

Like many women, she struggled to make the union with her husband a success. It was no storybook marriage, but the two of them found a way to make it work. It was, in the end, a marriage that found its footing and blessed all involved. Jacob and Leah learned, they grew, and they became the couple they needed to be for themselves, their family, and most of all, their God.

Many women find themselves without the dream marriage and life they originally desired, but God is available to provide purpose and a path. He continues to love, and he continues to guide, if we but listen and follow his direction.

Tamar lived the nightmare that so many women, before and after, fear and sadly many experience. Her rape at the hands of her half-brother Amnon was unexpected and unimaginable. The catastrophic sometimes happens in life, without warning or justification. Evil exists. Does God abandon, or is he still available for those who have experienced the unspeakable? At Tamar's darkest moment, her brother came to give her comfort. Absalom was no angel, but in that moment, he was an angel to his sister. In the words of one individual who had experienced great pain in his life, "God always sends somebody to help."

We must remember to look upward. God is there. Moreover God has given us all the opportunity and mission to stand in the gap for those who are voiceless and helpless. How can someone get back up when given a strong body blow that knocks them to their knees, and their heart as well as their body is cast down? How can someone, anyone hold their head up when they have been hurt, embarrassed, publicly held up for ridicule? How can someone keep going when there seems to be no hope?

There is much to learn from these imperfect lives.

ACKNOWLEDGMENTS

My thanks to all those who have helped in the creation of this book. I am especially thankful to Mrs. Nadine Holmes and Pastor Clarence Agard for their assistance and encouragement.

I continue to be grateful to the late Pastor Patricia Howard and Rev. Dr. John Berry, who always believed in this volume and encouraged me to write it.

I am also grateful to my family and especially, Bruce and Vernita Johnson, who in their short time here among us showed us what giving of one's self for others really means. Service to others defined both their lives. You continue to be an inspiration. You are missed.

PART I

Love Like A Leah

INTRODUCTION

Some people are never forgotten. Even in death, Jacob and Leah continue to help others navigate the sometimes confusing, invigorating, perilous, but always purposeful journey of life and love. They were buried in a cave 3,700 years ago, the Cave of Machpelah, as it is now known. The double cave was discovered beneath a building built during the second Temple Period (two thousand years ago) by Herod. It is a sacred site and has been, at various times, both a church and a mosque (Golding, n.d.). As such, it is dear to the heart of Jews, Christians, and Muslims. All three religions honor Abraham as a great man of God.

There lie the remains of a family. The matriarch was Sarah, the mother of many generations. She was a woman, resigned to be barren, childless to her own regret and sorrow, at least temporarily. In life, love, and matters of destiny, the pulse of God's timing does not always align with man's expectations. Near Sarah, there is Abraham, her husband, and there, in the quietness, can be found proof of God's faithfulness. There lies the child that everyone thought was impossible, everyone, that is, except those whose vision was empowered by faith and they were graciously permitted by God to glimpse the future. Isaac was, for them, the miracle baby. He was born to parents too old to bear a child. It was impossible, and yet it was possible through God's providence.

This gift of vision is not for everyone, but where there is great destiny, the Lord prepares in unusual ways. Abraham was such a man and was instrumental in God's plan. Isaac was the son who was hoped and prayed for and yet still came as a surprise to his mother, Sarah, who dared doubt God's Word. There lies Isaac. There, too, is his beloved wife Rebekah. This is a place of burial for the patriarchs and the women they loved.

In his great wisdom, God had Abraham purchase the burying place for his wife Sarah. God knew and Abraham understood that both Abraham and his descendants needed a place to call their own, where they could rest in death. Because of this, Abraham chose to buy rather than accept the cave as a gift when it was offered as such (Genesis 23:1–9).

The first wife of Isaac and Rebekah's son, Jacob, is also buried there. Dust upon dust, ashes upon ashes, there lies Leah, the faithful wife of Jacob. She was often misunderstood and frequently criticized, but today she is honored and respected as a woman of prayer and a matriarch of the Jewish and Christian faiths.

Some see her as a woman who lived in the shadow of Rachel. Even in death, Leah's virtues escape many, but the virtues were there in her heart and life. There also lies the man Leah loved, for surely a love of the strength and devotion that Leah possessed cannot be stilled by death. If any force can outlive death, it would be love, pure love, and unfailing love. It would be love tried by the fire of negative circumstances. It would be love defined as hopeless by those ill-informed and misled, but survives nevertheless. Love is rarely predictable, often surprising, and at its purest, stronger than steel with the softness of a new baby's skin. There lies the remains of the man Leah shared with her sister Rachel. There lies Jacob.

The location, the cave, is no doubt a quiet and sacred place. There Leah has had, for over two thousand years, her beloved to herself. Jacob's first love was known to all the ages to be Rachel. She was the Rachel who, in his eyes, never lost her beauty. She was the Rachel who cried out to God, "Give me a son or I will die." She was the Rachel whose life ebbed out in childbirth only after she saw her second child. The child was Benjamin, and she offered him as a remembrance of the love she shared with Jacob and the bitterness of having to leave her beloved after painfully and fatefully giving birth.

Years later, Benjamin's brothers knew the mere thought of losing this, the second son of Rachel, could cause their father to tremble in fear. The brothers tried to protect Benjamin in ways their jealousy prevented them from protecting Joseph. The partiality of their father extended to the children of his wives. The children of Rachel were favored, and none knew this better than the sons of Leah.

Joseph was the firstborn of Rachel. He was buried in Shechem on a piece of land that Jacob had purchased. It was Joseph who God permitted to be reconciled to his family. It was this Joseph who offered forgiveness to his brothers for what to some would be unforgivable. They sold him into slavery thinking they would never see him again, but God thought otherwise. Joseph observed that they meant it for evil, but God meant it for good (Genesis 50:20). The brothers had unwittingly been a part of God's plan to save his people. These brothers, Joseph and Benjamin, were dear to their father's heart just as Rachel, his wife, was dear to his heart. How strange it is that Leah would be the one who would rest with the beloved Jacob in death.

At last, at long last, Leah has Jacob to herself. It is she who is honored by his presence. What is it that Leah teaches us through her life? What does she teach us in her strength, her weakness, her longings, and her destiny? What can we learn from the faith that kept her going even after a painful error in judgment and possibly her deliberate deceit so that she could be with Jacob (Genesis 29:21–25)? Leah the less loved, Leah the less beautiful, and Leah the matriarch instructs on how to rise above circumstances, overcome failures, and encourages self-acceptance. She teaches each new generation how to find peace with God and their place in the world.

As Leah speaks through words and actions, listen. You will feel her spirit, and she will minister to everyone for she speaks out of the weight, pain, and joy of her own experiences, and she shares a story that only she can tell. Listen and hear her voice. Look, see, and understand not only her actions and decisions but your own and those around you. Like others in scripture, her story was written before time and for our learning that we might attend to the words and grow.

Many want to turn their heads from the possibility that this may not be a simple story of a jealous sister seeking to take away "her sister's man." That view keeps it simple and casts the entire story in a tabloid frame that is all too familiar. Many times, situations are not as simple as they appear on the surface. Leah has been held up as an example of a woman who would pay any price for a man, as a jealous woman, as a true daughter to her father, using deceit and trickery to achieve her own desires. There is more, much more, to the beautiful Leah.

Yes, in her own right she was beautiful. Open your heart to Leah's story, and you will hear the story of a thousand women who themselves will instantly understand who she is. Open your mind, and you will perceive her logic, sometimes deeply flawed, but nevertheless her logic. Open your spirit, and you will know that even those who have made poor decisions, have felt they were relegated to the second choice, the least desired, and the one that nobody noticed and you will see the transforming power of God at work. You will know that no matter the situation, condition, choices, characterization by the world around you that God, your maker and your most faithful companion, will use his creative power to give greater meaning, greater joy and fulfillment to his perfectly formed creation. The perceived flaws are the unique features that add value and distinctiveness to the precious jewel he has created in forming each and every person. Let Leah tell her story.

CHAPTER 1

Laban

It almost feels like a small-town drama, a biblical type of soap opera. For some, depending on age and background, it might be like *Peyton Place*, and for others *General Hospital* or *The Young and the Restless*. For still others, Latin telenovelas may come to mind. For those who grew up when soap operas ruled afternoon television, the love, the drama, the intrigue may feel like it came out of a well-written script, but instead it came straight from scripture. Today many people are absorbed in the activities of reality television (which in some cases might be called created reality), but this true story and many others found in scripture can rival the drama and excitement of anything that can come from the imagination of a Hollywood writer.

Laban was both a central and supporting character at various times in his life. His father was Bethuel, and his grandfather Nachor, an older brother to Abraham.

As is the case in many situations, someone who appears to be a minor player is found to have huge influence. This may well describe the influence of the praying and wise servant Eliezer. It was Eliezer who heard the voice of God and humbly sought the hand of Rebekah for his master, Isaac. His careful and wise actions were critical to the marriage that is pivotal in biblical history.

While not directly involved, at this point, Laban saw the drama unfold. He came to respect the God of Abraham, Isaac, Jacob, and his own sister Rebekah. There is no doubt Laban was aware of the wealth of Isaac's family based on what they offered for Rebekah. He was, in fact, related to Abraham himself. Laban was Abraham's great-nephew. His sister Rebekah was married to Isaac, so he was an uncle to Jacob. (Laban-chabad.org, n.d.).

When the time came for Jacob to leave his childhood home and family, the decision had to be made quickly so as to avoid any violence between the brothers, Esau and Jacob. The rivalry between the brothers started in the womb. At birth, Jacob was even born holding on to the heel of his brother Esau (Genesis 25:26). Jacob wanted his brother's birthright and finally, through deceit, an impulsive poor decision by Esau, the help of his mother, and outright trickery, Jacob was able to secure the blessing that was meant for Esau, the elder son (Genesis 25:27). Esau's realization of his loss of birthright and the anger at his twin were seen as potentially dangerous for both men.

The parents loved both their children and decided that Jacob could go to Rebekah's childhood home, where Eliezer first saw Rebekah, and she agreed to marry Jacob. Her family could be trusted. Rebekah knew she could count on her brother to help mentor her son and help him to marry the right bride. Family was and is central to a person's life and development, be it the biological or chosen family. In the end, these are the people who know and love a person and, for many, the people who celebrate their birth, mourn their passing, and keep an invisible candle in their heart for the rest of their lives. It burns with vivid memories long after others have forgotten a person's face and name, long after the physical remains have become unrecognizable as the person they once were. It is long after the person who once breathed in deeply, smiled, laughed with joy, and returned love in tangible ways existed on this plane of reality. There are many who would insist that love continues. Maybe mere mortals cannot see it manifested as they once did, but if it is strong enough, perhaps that love still exists, giving hope and strength through the memories of those who knew them. Love makes a family, and family is everything.

Laban, in the tradition of his region and country, was welcoming to his nephew Jacob. Without knowing him, he did know him. Laban greeted Jacob with love. Visitors, in general, were to be treated with kindness and respect, how much more so a relative. From his earlier experiences with the family, Laban also knew that the family of Isaac was blessed. There is always a blessing in blessing the people of God. Laban later says as much in Genesis 30:27: "If now I have found favor in your eyes, stay here, for I have divined that Yahweh has blessed me for your sake."

Laban was open to Jacob and was willing to agree to an offer of marriage to Rachel. Laban's behavior and decisions as a direct result of this agreement helped to shape the negative impression many have of him. When Jacob proposed marriage to Laban's daughter, Laban agreed to Jacob's terms, and for seven years, there was no indication that Laban restated the terms of the agreement or indicated in any way that Jacob would not receive the hand of Rachel. There is no indication that he was not going to follow through. During those seven years, Jacob faithfully worked for his uncle, and because Jacob was blessed, his work was blessed, and in turn, Laban was blessed.

Laban was clearly observant and a good businessman. Jacob's presence meant increased blessings and greater wealth. They were family, so Jacob, while very quick and observant under normal conditions, may have let his guard down. As a one time deceiver himself, he was trying to follow a new path. Bethel had changed him. An encounter with the Lord always makes a difference. Jacob had a new focus in life. Oh, to be young and in love is a blessing. The time for Jacob passed quickly, as his love for Rachel was so great (Genesis 29:20). The time of the marriage went smoothly, and it is only after the consummation of the marriage that Jacob is aware of how he had been tricked. He awakened to find that the woman he had married was not Rachel but her sister Leah. He had consummated his marriage to the wrong woman!

It is at this point another side to the kind uncle Laban is exposed. Now it is clear why he was seen as a trickster and slickster. The question was not *if* he treated Jacob unfairly but rather why he did so. Some of the reasons for his behavior have a dark edge, a selfish quality. Others may be the result of being a father who really does desire the best for his daughters. Like many others, Laban was a complex person, and things were not necessarily the way they seemed.

Laban clearly tricked Jacob, and the end result was that Laban gained seven more years of service from him. Jacob had met his match in deceit and trickery, and the two would continue to find ways to try and get the upper hand over each other. There is little doubt that Laban knew that the older daughter should marry first but chose not to mention it in a timely fashion. This was clearly a case where the choice not to speak was a choice to create a climate of limited truthfulness that benefited Laban.

Failing to speak, in some situations, may well be just as powerful as uttering a false statement. It was not so much of a misunderstanding but more of a failure to provide information that was essential to the matter. Laban stood to gain, retaining not only a good worker but also a blessed worker. He held on to the daughter Jacob desired. This allowed Laban to continue to benefit from Jacob's labor. Laban was blessed because Jacob was there, but God also found a way to bless Jacob so that he would later leave prosperous.

After twenty years, Jacob wanted to move forward with his family and build a life apart from Laban. He and Laban, both cunning men, struck an agreement that would allow Jacob to build his own flock with spotted animals, separating them from the solid-colored animals of Laban. It seemed harmless enough at the time but, with Jacob's knowledge of animal husbandry, resulted in a great blessing for Jacob (Genesis 30:25–34).

Again and again, talented but insecure leaders hold on to mentees longer than they should so that they can continue to benefit from the mentee's talent, labor, and gifting. Some young men and women will just break away; others will work to be obedient and feel obligated to stay, even when the Lord has clearly spoken and their time at a ministry has come to an end. One minister shared that he went to the church where he was serving and physically could not unlock the door of the building. When he told the Lord, yes, he would take the next step, he would leave the congregation he loved and go to where the Lord was leading him, the key worked. He understood this to be a clear message that he should take the next step and leave the congregation he had grown close to so that he could take the next step. For a moment he forgot that no one including him, loved that congregation more than God and He was already working out their next step as well.

God's work is done through us with the work of our hands, but we are not to assume that we are the only ones he can use. If He (not our personal ambition) is directing us, then when it is time to move into another field, to begin something different, we should be obedient to his leading. God always knows what He is doing, even when we think we know best. We don't. We must lean on the Lord. God's work has to be done God's way and in his timing.

Regardless of Laban's intention, the years Jacob spent working with him did benefit Jacob. It was a time to build his family, to mature in his own right and build his own wealth. When Jacob went home, he was not the same, spiritually or naturally. After fourteen years working for his wives and six years working for his livestock, Jacob returned home a very different man from the one who had left.

The wife of Laban and the mother of Rachel and Leah is reported to be Adina (Moss, n.d.). Her name means "delicate." It is a beautiful name. There is not a lot of information available regarding Adina. She must have been a wonderful person. First, Laban chose her as his wife, and while something is known of Laban's character, we can only speculate about his wife based on her two daughters. What does it say of Laban that he chose a woman who bore such women of faith and love?

As a mother, Adina would have had an impact on the character of her daughters. In addition to being beautiful women, one more than the other, they were both loyal and faithful wives. They understood, probably as they had been taught, that there was a time when they were to be obedient to their father. They were to be good daughters who would help him and follow his direction, in their case, obedient even when the father's judgment was questionable. They also knew when to give that loyalty they shared with their father and even greater loyalty to their husband and their own families. While many do not know the mother's name, the names of her daughters, two matriarchs of the faith have been and continue to be known many years after their bodies have turned to dust. The sister wives were together in life, in good times and bad, but sadly separated in death, with only one to be buried with the beloved husband. They influenced the world through their sons, men whose names are known by Jews as well as Christians.

The work of a mother in instilling values, in teaching and directing her children, cannot be overestimated, but it can be undervalued. The work of a mother begins before the child is born, as this child will be a prayer charge as long as the parent and child live. Hopefully, parents will seek God together for their children, but regardless of the level of commitment from one parent or another, someone must pray that child through to their destiny. With so great a destiny for Leah and Rachel, some believe they had a mother who was diligent in daily teaching and training.

While Laban's decision-making can be called into question more than once, it might be that, in his own way, he loved his daughters also and felt he was looking out for their welfare (as well as his own). Some find it significant that he wanted Leah to have a week with her new husband before giving Jacob Rachel, the only wife he really wanted. Perhaps in a week, Jacob's anger would subside, and he would find a way to love Leah or at least not to hate her. He did not insist on putting her away, which suggests that in spite of his anger, he had compassion for her. For good or bad, Laban respected Jacob and was not releasing his daughters to someone he did not trust. He was releasing them to a man he felt would take care of them long after Laban was no more.

Laban valued and respected the God of Abraham based on his understanding of God's power to bring blessings to his sister Rebekah and to his own household. Like many of us, his own behavior may not have been consistent in terms of making right decisions. Knowing what is right does not always translate into doing right. Perhaps, like many individuals who understand but do not choose to do the right thing, at some point in his life, Laban recognized the importance of choosing the path of righteousness. Hopefully, even after the tense last encounter between Laban, his daughters, and son-in-law, Laban chose not only to respect the God of Abraham but also to cast aside the household gods, the false gods, and turn to the true and living God. Before discounting the possibility, consider the many who were counted out as unredeemable and changed course, including perhaps even Jacob.

CHAPTER 2

Leah

The Older Sister

During Leah's time, there is no doubt that male children were preferred and highly valued for many reasons, among them the fact that male children could contribute to the family in terms of doing harder work and the fact that in many cultures the family name would be continued with male children. When there are both male and female children, usually, the oldest male continues to be preferred. Nevertheless, in the event of two or more female children when there are no males, the oldest female did receive certain preferences. It is interesting to note that Laban did not mention the custom of the oldest marrying first until seven years after the initial agreement and then only when his deception was discovered. Had the tricky Laban already anticipated what would happen and wanted to extend the services of Jacob, who was obviously blessed, and thus brought a blessing to Laban's house?

Laban insisted that the older daughter must marry first. It would not be unusual in this area of the world for such a custom to exist. The custom would be a normal and an expected course of events. Jacob, no doubt, recognized this fact and may even have had a flashback of sorts to his own actions, when confronted with Laban's excuse for the switch. After all, it was Jacob who tricked his older brother out of the birthright. While we do not know for certain, it is altogether possible that, in the intervening seven years, Jacob might have mentioned to his uncle how he came to visit. It is even possible that he might have mentioned the circumstances of his departure from his own home, in other words his deceit of his own brother and the fact that he had received Esau's blessing from Isaac.

Jacob had taken the privilege of being the firstborn from his own brother Esau, and now he is forced to respect the tradition and practice in regard to Rachel and Leah. Instead of taking the privilege of birthright away, he is forced to honor it. When Jacob became aware of the switch, he was livid. He has been cheated. He asked for Rachel and received her sister. Perhaps God brought to his mind the pain his own trickery brought to his family. The scripture does not say, but it would be an irony hard to miss for someone as quick as he was. If Laban was aware of Jacob's background, Laban probably knew that this reminder would cut deeply.

Leah was the firstborn. This was actually a positive event, since coupled with her lesser beauty, lesser status might have made marrying her to a desirable son-in-law even more difficult for Laban. In a culture where being the oldest carries status, Leah had to feel the pain of the social comments that were, no doubt, made. It was Leah who should have been noticed and regarded more highly. Her beautiful sister was certainly noticed while Leah was probably just the sister.

This situation continues to occur in households everywhere. One child is effervescent, beautiful, charming, and other siblings feel relegated to the background. Perhaps the child's appearance is less striking, or their interest in sports, dance, music, you name it, not as pronounced. Perhaps one child shines academically. In these cases, parents must make a special effort to make sure that all the children know that they are valued and loved for who they are. They, like Leah, bring their own special uniqueness to the world. This uniqueness must, too, be celebrated. Like Leah, their true strengths may take longer to develop and blossom, but they must see themselves not in the shadow of another but casting their own shadow.

When Leah heard others speak of Rachel's beauty, by inference, they were also speaking of Leah's lack of beauty in their eyes. Did the sisters grow up with people making the distinction between the pretty one and her sister? The biblical text does not reveal any male suitors for Leah, but clearly Rachel was admired and well loved. Jacob asked for Rachel's hand, the younger daughter, but who would ask for the older sister Leah's hand? Surely, she too desired marriage, but no mention is made of someone seeking her hand in marriage.

Was it Leah who brought to her father's attention the fact that the younger should not precede the older in marriage? Was Laban seeking a way to extend Jacob's service? Was he trying to get rid of a daughter who was aging with no man showing interest? Was this a father who loved his daughters and was trying to help them both find a good husband and help himself in the process?

Laban's actions present a dilemma. Laban is a somewhat complicated personality. There is no clear indication of exactly when he conceived the plan to replace one bride with another. The fact is he did, and it was trickery worthy of Jacob himself. Laban was also quick to recognize what God promised Jacob at Bethel: wherever he went, Jacob would be blessed. Laban could see that Jacob's presence in his home was a blessing to Laban and his family.

Jacob negotiated again. Laban would give Jacob Rachel, but he had to work seven more years. His debt would be paid with seven years of labor. Rachel would be his second bride but only after Leah had a week for her own celebration with her husband. It is highly doubtful that it felt like a celebration, but at least, she had that week.

Again, there is no way to know what was going on in the mind of Laban. There is no way of knowing if Laban had planned this action all along or if he recognized the love of Leah for Jacob and sought not just to find her a husband but someone she truly loved as well. This point is especially interesting since, as Jacob and Laban bargained the second time, Laban made sure that Leah would have a week with her husband before the second marriage, this time to Rachel. Perhaps Leah could find some place in his heart in that week.

We do not know Laban's standing in the community, but we do know that his moral behavior was somewhat wanting. Did this behavior influence the decision of his daughters to go along with the marriage deception, or were they simply obedient daughters who did not express their own will? There is much here that raises questions, but one can be sure that it would not be likely that the daughters would openly oppose their father. This would be a behavior that would be unacceptable in their culture.

Leah may have been the oldest, but where Jacob was concerned, Rachel was the favored. Leah moves from being the less-attractive daughter to the less-loved wife when the marriage of Jacob and Rachel is consummated.

Regardless of his motives, Laban made sure both his daughters would be well taken care of and gave them both wedding gifts of value, handmaidens to take with them into the marriage. For all his shortcomings Laban appears to have loved his daughters. Leah would have a husband, and it was now up to her to build that relationship. Marriage was important for women. It was their destiny, and they needed marriage so they could bear and provide for children. Divorce was primarily a male privilege (Deuteronomy 24:1–3). If a man found out that his wife was not a virgin upon marriage or if she displeased him, he could obtain a divorce. A divorced woman faced the shame of her condition and the need to find another marriage partner.

Leah may have made a miscalculation. She took a chance, and it didn't work out as she may have hoped, but she moved ahead and worked at being a good wife, a faithful wife, and in the end may have won a measure of respect from her husband if not a measure of love. She was not the beautiful Rachel, but she was Leah, the woman with whom he rested in death.

Leah has strength, devotion, and a capacity to love that would have been a blessing to any marriage. History remembers her as the less loved but must also acknowledge that in her womb was nurtured Judah, the line from which the Savior came. God placed wonderful qualities of steadfastness and resilience in her and knew that they would be a blessing to Jacob in time. He loved the lovely Rachel with the fire and passion of youth. He remembered her even on his deathbed. How could he not as his life passed before him? She was the love of his life.

But it was Leah with whom he shared most of his life, with whom he had most of his children, and with whom he rested in death. God permitted the deception of the marriage and allowed Leah's suffering but never forgot her. Leah cried out to God, and he heard her and blessed her with many sons. She came to understand that favor with God does not completely eliminate pain. Sometimes pain must be endured, but God in his wisdom can use that pain to build patience and endurance, to deepen sensitivity to the needs of others, to strengthen the prayer life and draw people closer to him. He never, ever forsakes those he has chosen, those he loves and granted favor. Leah was a woman highly favored by God.

CHAPTER 3

Rachel
The Beloved

Rachel was Laban's second child, and she was a keeper of her father's flock, known to others in the village, who quickly pointed her out and identified her when Jacob was at the well. She was, by all accounts, the kind of girl who, as she grew into womanhood, was a wonderful person. She was clearly very striking, as the scripture describes her as being "beautiful in form and attractive." (Genesis 29:17b). Rachel's features were pleasant to the eye, and she had a shapely figure. Men naturally gravitate to a beautiful woman and especially one who has a pleasant personality. Sadly, many times, women assessed to be less beautiful are treated in a less caring and respectful manner.

In some traditions, Leah and Rachel are believed to be twins with Leah as the firstborn in much the same way that Esau and Jacob were twins, with Esau being the firstborn. Prior to her marriage and the jealousy Rachel showed toward her sister during the time of her barrenness, it appears they had a positive relationship. They were, after all, sisters at the end of the day. They shared many of the same memories. There is frequently a certain comfort in sharing what might be called continuity of memories. They remember the times they made mistakes and laughed. They remembered the good and bad that happened in the family. Sometimes the explanation required when talking to someone who doesn't know the background of a situation makes it less likely that the person might truly understand or fully appreciate what is being said. In Laban's case, the daughters had seen him act and react over a lifetime, so they had some idea of what to expect from their father in a given situation. They understood and tried to help and protect Jacob when necessary. When the household gods were stolen, Rachel didn't tell her husband. She didn't want to implicate him, knowing how her father would react.

Rachel had so much in her favor, and she clearly had the love of Jacob. She was the woman of his dreams, and he was willing to pay any price to have her as his own, but after their marriage, her happiness faded. She was loved no less, but her infertility was a cause of shame and sadness. She wanted to conceive a child. After all the years of waiting, the difficulty in conceiving a child seemed unbearable. The pressure was not only from the world around her spoken or unspoken, but it was also very personal, based on her own internal drive. Marriage in the ancient world was less about love than producing a family. A large family was a great blessing. Marriage was expected for a young woman or man and then children. Love, the great gift of her marriage, was a wonderful plus but in no way was required. Children, on the other hand, were essential.

It is interesting to note that three of the four matriarchs, a clear majority, had problems with conceiving a child. They were Sara (also known as Sarah), Rebekah, and Rachel. Did this delayed cry of their heart drive them to seek God in ways they might not have done otherwise? Did this experience increase their sensitivity to others, help build and strengthen them, to help make them into the prayerful and loving matriarchs they became?

We do know that God did have mercy and opened the womb of these women. The fruit of their womb was blessed, and their children were chosen to help shape the destiny of a nation. Some of the pressures Sara, Rachel, and Rebekah faced came from deep within themselves and their desire to bear children for the men they loved. In a time and place where the major expectation of marriage was children, these women found themselves with husbands who loved them but a society that looked down on them. Some men might have considered putting Rachel away, divorcing her, because she was childless, but we see no indication that Jacob considered this. In fact, what might have felt like one of the great tragedies of her life, being the second instead of the first wife of Jacob, might have had positive results for her, but instead it was a source of jealousy. The Lord opened

Leah's womb, and she was fruitful early in the marriage. Jacob had biological children to continue his legacy.

Then, as now, fertility was seen as a blessing in all areas of nature. It is necessary for the crops and life as we know it. Each generation brings new ideas, new advancements and each generation is necessary. Everyone finishes their course here and another moves up. If a person lives to be a hundred years old, it is a short time compared to eternity. As one generation leaves, another will step forth. For this reason, then and to a large degree now, bareness was and is a cause for sadness.

It was also common during this time in history for people to worship multiple gods. Some of these gods were female entities including Asherrah, the lady of the sea (Judges 6:24–32), and Ashtoreth, a Canaanite goddess (1 Samuel 7:3–4). Females were valued in their particular roles as propagators of life even as deities. As monotheism spread, this worship of the female deity was discouraged, but the obvious link between women, childbearing, and the continuation of culture and life continued.

During the time of Rebekah, infertility was frequently seen as a curse. Childless women were looked down on and pitied. It was only natural that Rachel sought God to open her womb. J. P. De-Whyte explains that in the Ancient Near East (which she sometimes abbreviated as ANE) fertility is highly valued:

> The agricultural setting of the ANE fostered a culture of fertility. The tragedy attributed to

infertility stems from the importance placed on the fertility of humans, animals and the land. This culture of fertility is also evident in the worship of major deities many of whom were essentially fertility gods. The divine connection to fertility was dominant. (De-Whyte, 2018, 271)

It is God and God alone who opens the womb of a woman so that she can bear children, and it is this same God who will close the womb of a woman so that she will be barren, unable to have children.

This longing to bear a child was not limited to one culture, but wherever childless couples are found there are women willing to pay any price, including their lives, to bring a child into the world. Such a woman was Mrs. Yaramati. After years of trying, Mangayamma Yaramati underwent in vitro. It was successful and she was able to have twin girls by cesarean in 2019. At seventy-four at the time and her husband at eighty-two, they were the oldest known couple to experience parenthood for the first time. They were extremely happy and excited. These babies were considered a gift and a blessing. Like many others, Mr. and Mrs. Yaramati just wanted to be parents (Tan & Dutta, 2019).

Within their own families, women during the time of Rachel did have some influence and power. As Rachel and her sister grew into womanhood, they were groomed and prepared to take on the role that would be expected of them. This would usually include authority in the household. Of special note regarding that authority is Sarah (Genesis 21:11). She wanted Haggai and her son out of her home, and they were sent away. God gave Abram some comfort regarding the matter, but the Lord was clear in directing him to follow Sarah's wishes. In any tribal culture, there are many responsibilities, and women had their work, as Rachel's role as a shepherdess shows. Women were valued. The tribe was dependent on their female population for the continuation of the group, because without children, the tribe could not continue. To some extent, they were also dependent on them for many of the cultural teachings of the group. Children must be taught their cultural values for the group values and beliefs to continue. While later much of the valued history was written and preserved, early on, there was great dependence on men and women to maintain that oral tradition and pass on the information critical to the culture and group.

Rachel was a loving woman, a praying woman, and a woman who knew how to cry out to God in pain for her children. She died in childbirth with her second son. She is known as a matriarch, a mother of the faith. Because of the time difference between the exile and the time of her own death, Jeremiah's description of her weeping as her children went into exile might well have not been a literal interpretation of the event but a strong figurative image. This woman sought God day and night with tears and pain, longing for her own sons. This woman gave her life in the birth of Benjamin. This Rachel was buried, it is believed, along the road the beaten, worn, and captive exiles passed. She cried out in pain and grief, just as she did in life, for her children, her descendants. A strong, sensitive, resilient, and persistent woman like Rachel would have mourned the suffering of her own people. If she could, she would have wiped their tears. She grieved and hurt for them as any mother would.

During her lifetime, Rachel was persistent and prayerful. She stood strong, asking God for the desires of her heart. She would not give up. She held on just as Sara and Rebekah had done before her, and God heard them all. God heard their sincere prayers and blessed them. Their examples, their faithfulness, has blessed the people of God ever since. The generations of children born of the travail and the suffering of the matriarchs will forever honor them. No tears went unnoticed, no prayer unheard.

Because of the prayers of God's people, the children born were gifts from God to both their mothers and history.

CHAPTER 4

The Sisters

We first hear of Leah in Genesis 29:16. She is the daughter of Laban and sister of Rachel. While all sources agree on the captivating beauty of Rachel, there is some discussion as to the true meaning of the passage regarding Leah. She is described in the King James Version as "tender eyed." Other translations reflect other various shades of meaning:

- *New International Version*—"weak eyes"
- *New Living Translation*—"pretty"
- *New Revised/Good New Translation*—"lovely"
- *Complete Jewish Bible*—"weak"
- *The Bible in Basic English*—"clouded"
- *Young's Literal Translation*—"tender"

Should we turn to the dictionary? In that case, we get other shades of meaning for *tender*, which would include "compassionate or delicate." Were Leah's eyes dull, were they sensitive or weak, or were they beautiful? After an examination of the text, it would appear that while Leah may have had attractive eyes, Rachel's complete beauty was so overwhelming compared to the appearance of Leah that there was no mistaking the fact that the younger sister was by far the more desirable when it comes to physical beauty. To say that Rachel was more beautiful is not to say that Leah was unattractive. It is to say that Rachel was more so. There are many around the world who can immediately identify with living in the shadow of a more talented or, in this case, more attractive sibling. Frequently, it is the younger sister or brother who feels pressured to live up to the physical prowess, academic talent, or perhaps the magnetic personality of an older sister or brother. There is a need to separate, to distance oneself and try to be accepted as an individual, not as the little sister or brother who must fight to be accepted for being themselves. There is a struggle to avoid living in the shadow of someone else. A shadow may cast a bit of shade and cover, but it also blocks out the light that is so necessary to establishing one's own identity and place in the world.

An additional perspective is provided by Tzvi.

> The name Leah means tired and exhausted. The implication is that she is "sick and tired of life." Our first impression of Leah, therefore, is of a woman who is not particularly adaptable and accepting of life and her situation. She cries her eyes out, literally, about the potential match between her and

Esav, and her name denotes a basic dissatisfaction
and weariness with life (Tzvi, 2021).

Many believed that there was an arrangement that
Leah marry Esau and Rachel marry Jacob. Leah had no
interest in such a match. This view of Leah as a woman
whose tears were offered to God, as well as her prayers,
is shared by Kadari. "Accordingly, her weak eyes teach of
Leah's good traits: that she did not want to be married to
Esau" (Kadari, 2022). Esau had placed little value on the
privilege of the blessed place God wanted to give him. He
gave up something of great value for something of very
little. This was not the kind of man with whom Leah wanted
to share her life. Leah asked God to change this part of her
destiny. God answered her prayers but not in the way she
might have expected.

Frequently, the path God had designated for someone
seems to unfold like a mountain path with unexplained
twists and turns. This writer remembers driving up a
mountain path with a group of singles. There was a need
to appear calm, but inwardly, there were prayers for God
to keep the van on the road and keep everyone safe. It was
uncomfortable for someone who didn't like heights to drive
a vehicle with the lives of others in her hands. There was
a similar experience when attending a ministry workshop
on a cold and snowy day in a city that was over sixty miles
from home. The drive there was careful and cautious, but at
the end of the day, on the way back, the weather worsened.
There were cars to the left and right that had ended up

in accidents or were unable to continue on the icy and dangerous highway. Some had simply slid off the road and were just stuck. The group made it home safely but not without continual prayer during the drive. Now that was more of a challenge than any driver needed. It was a real faith journey! The uncomfortable reality is that sometimes the lesson is in the journey. Growth and maturity can be painful. There can be twists and turns, but God can use our mistakes, our wrong decisions to help build us into the people he means us to be.

This lesson was a hard truth. Leah's tears were many. Leah was learning how to seek God on levels that might not have been imagined before. Leah's sister Rachel is eternally associated with the lament recorded in Jeremiah 31:15. There may be times when we feel what we are being asked to do is too hard, too much, and we ask God to change the path, stop the pain, lift the burden. God hears our prayers, but a change does not mean the new challenges will be easier. Leah's destiny and place in history were set, and the journey to that destiny would not be easy or without tears and struggles. When we ask God to "Use me for your glory," we must be prepared to go through some difficult and challenging times. We must hold on tightly to His hand and always remember that He is bringing us out and that He is teaching us as we go through the pain and suffering.

Being known as the one who was less beautiful was a burden that Leah carried all her life. Even now when we speak of the sisters, we make the distinction between the one who was beloved and beautiful and the other wife. While any positive physical features she had were outweighed by the captivating beauty of Rachel, Leah had her talents, but sometimes people are too busy comparing one to another to really notice the uniqueness that every person has. Many women and men will stare in a mirror, studying their features and wondering how to cover what they perceive to be flaws and faults with makeup. If they have the disposable income, they may choose to undergo elective surgery to alter their features, not because of some physical abnormality but because a smaller nose, wider eyes, ears set closer to their head or even hair extensions will make them better, more attractive. Perhaps it will, and only they can weigh the costs and risks versus the possible end results. Only the individual can decide if it is appropriate for them. It is well to remember that there will always be someone more beautiful, and if all of a person's self-worth is built around physical beauty, there will be disappointments. As with Leah, being less beautiful does not mean there is no beauty. Our value to God and to those who love us is based on more than physical appearance and attributes. Each person has inherent value from God that no one can take away. Every person has worth. Every person has value, and more than that, there is a creator God who loves each and every one of his creations. Open your eyes and your lives to him. He is waiting. Others may see someone living in the shadow of another person but trust God. He will bring his children into their own.

There were probably many who saw the young women and remarked, "See, over there, there is Rachel, the beautiful daughter of Laban. He is blessed to have such a daughter who many men will want to marry. Oh, the other girl? That's her sister Leah. They don't really look like sisters." Laban will find someone to marry her, but Rachel is the real prize."

Throughout the Bible, women are mentioned for their beauty, their wisdom, their talents, their loyalty, and in the case of Jezebel, even their deceitful and wicked nature. Leah is different. The writer goes out of his way to let us know of her lesser beauty when compared with her sister. She was the older, less attractive sister. This, in itself, raises questions. Why is this information important? How can this information serve the reader? Did her lack of beauty have a bearing on her life?

If she were around during the twenty-first century, would her friends urge her to save her money for nips, tucks, implants, and liposuction so that she might attract some rich young man and be able to leave her father's home. Would she be encouraged to attend self-improvement classes so that she could learn how to attract people to herself. Perhaps a wardrobe makeover would help. Contacts might help those eyes, make them more attractive, a new hairstyle, new color, or just new hair altogether might make the difference. If she is to attract the right person, she needs to get about the business of making herself more than just average. Would everyone try to fix her? How critical is Rachel's beauty compared to Leah's less attractive appearance? How does Leah's appearance help to shape her? Leah had to know, just as we know, when people meet us and are disappointed?

Sometimes, individuals like Leah may have their positive qualities overshadowed by someone else whose total appeal is obvious and powerful. A young man may speak to a shy young woman as his eyes wander about the room looking for someone more striking. She stands there, ashamed for no reason other than she is who she is. Just like Leah, others know when they are rejected for something cosmetic, visual.

Perhaps like many others, Leah thought, if Jacob would take time to know her, he would find out who she really was. He could love her, maybe not in the same way he loved Rachel, but love nevertheless. There is reason to believe that Jacob did learn to appreciate Leah for who she was as the marriage wore on and he learned to know and appreciate her as a total person. His love for Rachel would always be present, but there is reason to believe he begins to see and understand Leah also.

Tamar Kadari notes in "Leah: Midrash and Aggadah" that one tradition asserts that while initially Jacob did not want to marry Leah, as he grew older, he described her as being the head of his bed, meaning she was the chief wife ("Leah: Midrash and Aggadah," n.d.). Like many couples, the beginning of their marriage was challenging, and at times, they might have questioned its survivability. But as the sisters found peace with each other and even, at times, a certain alliance, so did Jacob and Leah find themselves more at peace. Regardless of what was happening in the marriage, the marriage continued. Jacob and Leah continued. During Leah's years of fertility, they bore children together. The death of Rachel was a great loss to them both, and their common grief might have served to further bind them. Upon her death, Leah was provided a place of honor as her final resting place. As with many marriages, there were troubled days and years, but somehow through it all, the marriage survived and provided some level of companionship and comfort.

A review of the rabbinical literature sheds further light on Leah, the tender eyed (Hersch, 1906). When Jacob and Rachel met, Rachel told Jacob she had an older sister and that her father was capable of trickery. Jacob felt himself equal to the challenge of the situation, and he and Rachel agreed upon a sign that would identify Rachel when the marriage was to be consummated. Could it have been a particular piece of jewelry worn, a motion of the hand or both hands? It would be something that assured the groom that the heavily veiled bride was the woman of his dreams. Could it be that Rachel shared the sign with her sister? Leah could then use the sign to trick Jacob and fulfill the wishes of her father. If she did share the sign, it might well be an act of sisterly love. Without that sign, Leah might have been rejected and publicly disgraced. The elder sister would have faced public humiliation at what should have been a happy and joyful time, her marriage to Jacob.

Another question to be considered has to do with the terms elder and younger. Were the terms strictly a description of birth order for the sisters, or did it signify something greater? Was Leah not only the elder in birth order but also the elder in spiritual gifts? As we examine the hereditary lines, we see that Rachel's descendants, Saul and Joseph, were royalty but only for a season. On the other hand, Leah's descendants experienced it on a permanent basis. Jesus was a descendant of the House of Judah—Judah, the son of Jacob and Leah. Both women are loved and respected. Both have a place in history for their contributions to the faith.

Both Leah and Rachel were prophetesses. The rabbi makes this point in a response to a question that was asked on *Ask the Rabbi*. In the rabbi's words, "Both Rachel and Leah were prophetesses. For example, Leah foretold that Reuven would lose his birthright to Yosef, and that Reuven would try to save Yosef's life" ("Accounting for the Prophets," n.d.).

This raises more questions. Could Leah see her future role in Jewish history? Could this knowledge help to give her strength as she continued to struggle for acceptance in her challenging marriage? Could the knowledge that God had a place in history for both her and Rachel help to sustain her through the difficult times?

Contemporary believers have the benefit of the history of the faith, the stories of deliverance. There is so great "a cloud of witnesses." In her prophetic role, we do not know what the Lord revealed to Leah, but we do know that her prayer life as a woman who sought the heart of God as well as her sister's travail made a difference to all believers. God used these two women, matriarchs of the faith, to help fulfill the destiny of his people and his nation. Hindsight is always easier than the walk-through experience. These sisters made the best decisions they could, all of which could be put under the microscope dissected and analyzed, but to do so could only be helpful if we are using lessons learned to help us as we take our own walks of faith. They were women who helped to pave the way for the rest of us, and so we learn from them and grow from their decisions both good and questionable.

Could Leah see the role both she and her sister were to have in Jewish history? Did Esau's early behavior in taking his birthright so lightly concern her? Did God release her from this destiny and allow her to share her husband in the marriage to Jacob? These questions have been examined and reexamined by rabbis throughout the ages. The events are there to teach us as we walk our own unique path in the world.

When Jacob's family left Laban's household and country, Rachel caused confusion by stealing the household gods. The gods were idols believed by some to have power. Why would Rachel take the gods with her? It is possible that just as a young person moving away from home for the first time might want some keepsake to remind them of home, she might have taken them for that reason. It could be that both women were upset with Laban regarding their inheritance. Perhaps taking the gods was a spiteful act. Another possibility is that the gods themselves may have been felt to have power. Rachel would not want the gods to reveal the family's route or destination to Laban. Some writers feel that the gods would somehow help to prove their inheritance should that need arise. There is also the noble possibility. Rachel may have wanted her father to put his idol gods away and, to help him move in the direction of worshiping the true and living God, she removed the gods from his possession. We are not provided a clear-cut answer to this question. We do see behavior that clearly reminds us of the men in her family.

Her response to Laban when Jacob gave him permission to search his property for the gods was what one might expect from Laban himself. Knowing that her father would not want any part of touching a woman during that time of the month, Rebekah hid the items and then declared herself to be unable to move out of her saddle as she was in her unclean time. His second daughter, like her husband and her father, had the ability to think quickly and use shades and mixtures of truth.

The sisters had some tense and trying moments but managed to come together in spite of their problems. They knew who they were. They both wanted the best for Jacob, the man they both loved.

Rachel and Leah were chosen to play critical parts in the history of God's people, they both had God given insight on some of the situations that surrounded them. If Leah knew of Jacob's blessings and promise at Bethel, how much more would she desire to share her destiny with a man favored by God. It is difficult, if not impossible to determine the degree to which Leah was just obeying her father, as an obedient daughter, and the degree to which she may have desired to see this marriage move forward and her father's behavior just provided a means to achieve the desired end. She would not have wanted to hurt her sister, but now they both needed to obey their father at a time when girls and women just did not ordinarily challenge their fathers or husbands. What woman would not want to be married to a kind and wealthy man. Perhaps her own secret desire was for this marriage to work. Leah and her sister would later struggle with their places in the marriage. It is clear that jealousy and envy played a part in their relationship and marriage to Jacob, but there is little reason to doubt that they cared for each other. The matriarchs were a gift to us all, but their place in history came at great costs to them both.

They were chosen, and they accepted their place in history. It was a decision that shaped their lives and is far too complicated to be reduced to just "the wives." God chose women who he knew were worthy of the blessed position they would hold for the people of God. Abraham, Isaac, and Jacob have unique places in the heart of believers. To fulfill their destiny, God prepared the women all of them needed in their lives. Sara, Rebekah, Leah, and Rachel would face great challenges. They were indeed women of God.

CHAPTER 5

God Meant It for Good

The story of Leah and her sister Rachel cannot be told without intertwining it with Jacob's own personal history. Several questions immediately come to mind. Why did he leave home? How did he come to be in another country among his relatives? Was there any consequence for his own poor decision in acquiring his brother's birthright through deception? Jacob's journey was neither simple nor easy, but to his credit, he grew in the process and became the man God meant him to be.

God has a way of choosing the right person who may look like the wrong person to those who dare try to understand the logic of God. How often has God used the most improbable person to achieve the goal he desires? It is highly unlikely that anyone would have suggested Saul of Tarsus as one of the most significant missionaries of all time, someone who would be a martyr for Christ. Esther, a Jew, would become Queen of Persia and is able to save her people from destruction—unthinkable. Jacob was not the perfect son or brother, but God had an assignment for him that required an "extreme makeover." This was more than cosmetic. This was truly a change from the inside out.

The younger son of Isaac and Rachel, Jacob had no interest in being the number two son with the number two blessing (Genesis 25:24–26). Jacob, the cunning and quick thinker, sought and received what he wanted. He was the favorite of his mother. One day Esau was tired and worn out from his hunting and came home to find his brother preparing stew. Naturally, Esau asks for some of the food. Jacob quickly offered him a deal. Sure, he would trade the food, but in return, he wanted his brother's birthright, the privileges that went with being the firstborn. Faint and hungry, Esau unwisely agreed and ate his fill (Genesis 25:27–34).

Later Isaac, Esau's father, old and almost blind, realizing his days were coming to an end, asked Esau to kill and prepare some venison for him to eat, and he would give Esau the blessing of the firstborn. Rebekah heard the conversation. She quickly decided to help Jacob. She prepared savory lamb that was cooked just the way Isaac liked it. She instructed Jacob to dress in Esau's clothes. Rebekah then made him a pair of gloves from the hairy skin of the goats and put a strip of the hide around his neck. She helped to disguise Jacob as Esau so that Isaac could be deceived. This way he could bless Jacob thinking he was blessing Esau.

Rebekah and Jacob had to act quickly to complete the deceit before Esau returned from hunting and preparing his father's food. The two could not afford to be discovered before the deceit was completed. They were successful, and Isaac, with his poor vision, unknowingly gave the blessing meant for the firstborn to Jacob. He received the blessing his father meant for the eldest son through trickery (Genesis 27). No doubt charming and engaging, Jacob learned to use his wit and charm to secure what he wanted. Jacob supplanted his older brother, receiving the blessing that was meant for Esau. His mother was an active player in this web of deceit, and they both failed to realize the full impact of their actions. As frequently happens, they saw the short-term results and the possibility of getting what they wanted. That was all that mattered. What about the long-term impact on both themselves and others?

Modern history has its share of people who used deceit and then lost far more than they ever gained. Charles Ponzi, for whom the Ponzi scheme was named, defrauded thousands but died in a charity hospital with seventy-five dollars for his burial (Carlton, 2020). Bernie Madoff, who many feel perfected the Ponzi scheme, stole millions but lost everything that he cared about, including his wife and children. He died in a prison, still hated by thousands of people (Balsamo, 2021). These are just two of many, but as always, the master of deceit works to convince someone of the impossible—your secret sin will remain secret and there will be no price to pay. Sadly, there are those who still listen and are still convinced by the words they want to hear and the path that seems like an easy way out. We do not know if either Ponzi or Madoff found the right path and the peace they needed. We can only hope they did.

Some, like Jacob, allow God to do great works in their life. Pastor Scotty West is such a person. From a young age, he was involved in many forms of white supremacy. He served prison time for fighting, gambling, stealing, cooking drugs, doing drugs, and recruiting young people to join him in the white supremacy movement. While in a California prison in 1998, he reported that Jesus came to him and directed him to a Gideon Bible that was on the shelf. Scotty read John 10:10, asked God into his life, and was never the same man again. He started a Bible study class while still in prison and continued to do evangelistic work after his release. He became a pastor and also founder and director of four drug-and alcohol-recovery rehabilitation homes (Driscoll, 2005). Like Jacob he turned things around.

The Bible record provides the path and the growth of Jacob so that we may not only learn but be encouraged that, no matter our start, if we humble ourselves and turn, God can and will use us in his service. The Lord will give us favor. Just as the sunset follows the sunrise, there are consequences to acts and decisions, but with God's help, we will make it through to the other side. Jacob had to leave his home and start over in a distant land. That was, however, only the beginning. A new phase of his life began when Isaac blessed Jacob and sent him away to Paddan Aram. Isaac and Rebekah had reason to fear Esau's anger after the horrible deception perpetrated by mother and son. Esau's response was predictable, but because Jacob and his mother were so focused on their own goals, they failed to appreciate how much damage their deceit would cause. Neither of Jacob's parents could bear the thought of their own children replaying the horrible fate of Cain and Abel (Genesis 4:8). There is no reason to doubt they knew the story of Cain's deceit and the murder of Abel. They did not want to lose either of their precious sons. The mother who helped her son deceive his father must now work with him to help her favorite son survive. While Jacob had willfully stolen the birthright of his brother, it was not for Esau to resolve the situation. God would deal with Jacob's correction.

Isaac instructed Jacob in Genesis 28:5 to seek a wife not among the Canaanites but rather from the place where Isaac had been blessed to find Rebekah. That was in the house of Bethel. Jacob was to go to his mother's brother, Laban. Isaac and Rebekah were, no doubt, aware of Laban's daughters. Jacob's parents understood that marriage was more than just an opportunity for companionship and to build a family. It could, with the right person, help to move someone closer to or further from the will of God.

Jacob, at this point, may not have fully understood the necessity of joining one's body, mind, and spirit to the person God ordained rather than the person of convenience or carnal charm, but it is certain his parents wanted the best for him. It is certain they understood. Isaac sent Jacob where, in his own spirit, he knew his son would find the right wife. Surely, God would find a way to bring blessings out of this terrible situation. Jacob had to find and marry the women who would prove to be the right women to mother the destiny of a nation. Realizing that his father gave him specific instructions that should be followed. Jacob was obedient and began the journey that would alter his life and his character and clarify his destiny.

Jacob would inherit the promises given to Abraham, but Jacob's journey to his destiny required refining, growth, maturity, and a dependence on and obedience to God that could not be compromised. It would not be easy. That same persistence and cunning that had caused him trouble in the past would now work in his favor as he allowed God to guide him.

How often do people hold great spiritual potential and promise but squander them on selfish, personal goals rather than being faithful and obedient to God? It could be a brilliant computer expert who uses his talent to embezzle from a company instead of helping to spread the gospel with the internet, or a talented performer who confuses talent that is a gift from God with something that they personally own and, therefore, misuses that talent for personal fame/gain. It might even be a brilliant orator whose gifts were meant for the pulpit but instead were used to misguide, misuse, and exploit others. Some give up so much to gain so little for eternity. Jacob truly stood at a crossroad in his life. Which way? How would he proceed? His choices would shape his future.

In a real sense, Jacob was at the beginning of his own critical journey. He fled with little, and so he was forced when he reached Bethel to make a pillow out of stones to rest his head for the night. In those hard times for him, God spoke truth to Jacob's heart in a dream (Genesis 28:11–16). How fitting that when faced with harsh conditions, Jacob could quiet himself and hear the voice of God telling him how he would be blessed. He saw a ladder from heaven to earth, angels ascending and descending, and the Lord himself addressed Jacob. The place where Jacob was sleeping on the hard earth would be his and his descendants'. His descendants would be impossible to count, like the dust, spread in all directions. God would send them all. No one said it better than Jacob himself in Genesis 28:16: the Lord was there, and he didn't know it. Perhaps most important of all to Jacob during this uncertain time was the promise in verse 15. God was with him, here, now, and forever, and God would fulfill every word that he had promised to Jacob. Jacob felt the blessing of God and knew he had to somehow honor and remember this time. He set up stones for a pillar. He wanted to build a monument when he came back to this place. He built an altar and poured oil on it.

If the average person were invited to visit a head of state, be it a queen, king, president, or prime minister, they would make sure they were prepared to look their best. They would be on their best behavior and probably take pictures to preserve the moment. How much more so with God. To be in his presence is a precious time to be remembered and treasured. Jacob had to worship, as do all who experience God's presence. How could one do otherwise? Each opportunity to worship is a blessing. It is a time to praise God but also to listen to His voice and understand what he is saying to direct and guide. Private devotions are often seen as boring and avoided by many who have not discovered the simple truth of God's presence. Once experienced, one wants to return, to rush to that time and place, to open the heart and share the burdens of the day, to come as Jacob with nothing but oneself to offer before the Lord and to see, to feel, to know that God is in the place with you.

He is there in your prayer closet, in your home, in your secret place to worship. He is there in a tiny house church with only one or two members. He is there in a great cathedral with thousands. He is there to meet us when we come with open hearts and a desire to know him. The Lord is always there waiting to hear the voice of his creation, crying out to him, and most of all, praising him and thanking him. The Lord is there for the little boy or girl who whispers the now-I-lay-me-down-to-sleep prayer, the homeless people on the street with no place to go, the abused wife, husband, or child. Each of our voices is distinct, and no whisper is too low, no cry too pained, no person so insignificant that He will not attend to their cry. The Lord is in your place of worship right now just as he was there for Jacob. Look up and you will see the angels attending to your needs. You, like Jacob, may feel alone, abandoned, or fearful, not knowing what the future holds, but stop at your Bethel and commune with God. You have a future and a hope. You have a Father God and a Savior in Jesus Christ who is waiting for you. Look up and see God.

Whatever his fears and doubts after Jacob's time of communion with the Lord, he is ready to go forward. The fear has been replaced with hope and encouragement. The spirit of worship is in his heart as he moves back into the world, as he moves forward in the destiny God has assigned for his life.

Jacob's journey takes him next to the well. Did he remember the love story of his parents and how and where they met? We do not know for sure, but his steps are ordered by God, and he is now a man who is willing to follow the path God has set for him. Jacob had come to a new place, not only physically but spiritually as well. He is moving forward in every sense of the word. He may look the same. He may not have any more money or materials possessions, but the time at Bethel made all the difference in his life.

CHAPTER 6

Encounter at the Well

Water has great significance both in scripture and life. Without water, life would be impossible. Civilizations have long developed and flourished near water sources. Throughout history, even until today, water is not just used for drinking, but for fishing, transportation, and even for watering crops. Water was and is essential.

As a life-giving force, ancient people were drawn to water. They frequently gathered at the water source, making it both a social gathering place and a place to collect water to take home for drinking and cooking. In some cultures, members of the community gathered for washing clothes, personal hygiene, and for recreation. Whenever someone thinks of waterfalls, rivers, and oceans, this life-giving force can bring powerful images to mind. The beaches, the lakes, and streams are sources of recreation, enjoyment, and peace. In today's world, water frequently serves as a source of hydroelectric power in many areas, providing the necessary power for electricity. Many small communities and churches still use rivers for baptisms and other cultural rituals. There is no question that water is critical both for life and symbolism in matters of faith. For those who have experienced floods and the threat of angry waves, there is also a respect for the power and destruction that water can also bring.

Water is first mentioned in scripture in the book of Genesis and last in the book of Revelation and hundreds of times in between. The importance of water both to natural and spiritual life is seen throughout scripture. In Genesis 1:20, life comes from water. In Exodus 17:6, Moses strikes the rock to bring forth the living water for the children of Israel. In Ephesians 5:26, the church is washed by the word, invoking an image that all can understand. So strong, in fact, is the image of water in the Word that when the term *living waters* is mentioned, it immediately invites the listeners to make that association between the natural water that springs up out of the earth unfiltered, pure, cool, and satisfying and that which comes from heaven, that spiritual blessing that can come like a drenching rain on dry, parched earth desperately needing moisture. Taking in that much-needed natural or spiritual water is like drinking deeply from an untainted mountain stream. It is both refreshing and renewing. It is just what is needed at the time it is needed. Life and hope spring from living water. Renewed purpose and direction spring from living waters. Having once tasted the living water, nothing else quite satisfies.

The woman at the well was changed forever. She could not find what she needed from multiple husbands. Surely, they gave a sense of happiness for a moment, but the thirst kept coming back. The restlessness kept coming back. She was not entirely sure what she needed and wanted. She just knew that no one was enough. There was still an unquenchable thirst, a continuing need and longing. The reason Jesus needed to stop by the well was not so much about physical water but more about providing the living water that was so badly needed. The woman drank deeply and could hardly wait to share her discovery with others. One sip of good, fresh water changes a person's perspective of what water should taste like. One sip of spiritual water does the same. She was seeking, not entirely sure what she needed and wanted. She just knew that there had to be more. She needed living water. Living water is springing up, bubbling, running. Living water is active and fresh. Many suggest that there is quite a difference between the living water mentioned earlier and the water to be found in many of our municipalities. It is purified, chlorinated, and sometimes even flows through pipes that alters its usefulness or taste or both. The water from a mountain stream seems somehow more alive, more vital. While the latter is certainly useful and able to support life, the first is so preferred that many will buy bottled spring water to drink.

The woman at the well inquired of the Christ regarding this living water, the water that refreshes, consoles, that springs up in our souls and covers the dry, parched areas of our lives with the soothing reality of the Lord's presence, comfort, and new life. She, as we, need that living water.

How appropriate that at this time of a new beginning, Jacob should come to this place in the community, the place of the well. It was a gathering place. Like his father, Isaac, Jacob has a life changing encounter that began at a well. While his father's servant found the beloved Rebekah there at the well, Jacob comes for himself to be refreshed and to find his relatives. The theme of water is central to both their lives as their time comes to find a spouse draws near. The living water, the flow of God's spirit in their lives, the refreshing and renewing experience of love. It will all start at the well for them, the source of water, the source of life.

The theme of water goes back to the time of Abraham when he wanted to find the right wife for his son Isaac.

Abraham's servant, Eliezer, went to the spring. Everyone would come to the spring at one time or another. The servant prayed at the spring for God's direction:

> "Behold, I am standing by the spring of water. The daughters of the men of the city are coming out to draw water. Let it happen, that the young lady to whom I will say, "Please let down your pitcher, that I may drink," then she says, "Drink, and I will also give your camels a drink,'—let her be the one you have appointed for your servant Isaac. By this I will know that you have shown kindness to my master."

> Before he had finished speaking, behold, Rebekah
> came out, who was born to Bethuel the son of
> Milcah, the wife of Nahor, Abraham's brother, with
> her pitcher on her shoulder. (Genesis 24:13–15)

It had to be a woman willing to travel from her own country and family to start a new life in a new land. It had to be a woman willing to marry a man that she had not yet met. It had to be a woman who was able to exercise a measure of faith as she moved into her future. And God sent the young woman, later to become the love of Isaac's life, his treasured wife, Rebekah. Her spirit, attitude, beauty, willingness to help, and the response of her family all confirmed that she was God's choice for his servant, Isaac.

So often people use the expression "God is a right-now God," and this is one of those situations that illustrates that point. Eliezer prayed, and God responded at that moment to his request. God responds to the prayers of his people in ways great and small. Just as he answered the prayer when Eliezer prayed, he will do the same for us. The answer to the prayer was already in the making. Rebekah had already left her home and was on her way to get water, but she moved when prompted. This was her time to be blessed, and she had to be in the move of God.

Rebekah could have said to herself, "I need to get the water, but I have enough for now. I don't feel like going to the well. I think I will wait until later." She stopped whatever she was doing, picked up her pitcher, and started out to the well. Her pace was calibrated to place her there just in time to be that answer that God was sending. She might have stopped to talk to friends but she has a destination, a God-determined destination, and she had to be on time. She was going for water, but God was taking her to the beginning of a new life.

Never underestimate the importance of timely obedience. The answer to your prayer is coming. Just as we can be carried by the flow of a stream or river, we must stay in the flow of God, sensitive to where he is directing. When we do so, we will find ourselves at the right place at the right time to receive the blessing he has for us.

Isaac was blessed again and again, and he knew it and worshiped the God who made it so. The promise-keeping God, the dream-fulfilling God, the God who had never failed him, continued to walk with him and watched over his life. Even in the midst of the family turmoil, Isaac would continue to call upon the true and living God for direction, and God would work it out.

It was time for Jacob's departure. Isaac had been blessed from the house of Bethel, and perhaps God would now mercifully also bless his son Jacob. Like every parent, Isaac, no doubt, knew his children. He could see the potential for good. But he also knew that Jacob was a trickster. If he did not fully appreciate it before Esau's blessing was stolen, he did afterward. The favorite of his mother, Jacob was willing to push boundaries and take shortcuts for what he wanted. Sometimes shortcuts can be costly. Jacob, indeed, faced the painful lesson of what happens when self-interest is the only interest. Jacob wanted the privilege and rewards of being the firstborn and, with the help of his mother, successfully tricked Isaac into giving him the blessing meant for Esau.

After working seven years for the hand of Rachel, Jacob found himself tricked into marrying Leah, the firstborn. Tradition required that Leah was to marry first. This fact was never discussed in the marriage negotiations but simply thrust upon Jacob. The situation was eerily similar to his own trickery. Jacob had manipulated others to secure the rights of the firstborn that were due to his brother Esau. This time, however, Jacob's experience was from a completely different perspective. Instead of being the perpetrator, he is now the victim. Jacob probably felt cheated, not unlike Esau felt after his blessing was stolen.

As a father, Isaac had to pray that those character traits of persistence and determination remain but that they be turned toward and not away from God's will for his life. Isaac had to make sacrifices for his children and hold them up before the Lord. He had to ask for mercy and forgiveness. He had to intercede for them until they had the spiritual intelligence to seek God for themselves.

Isaac loved his children just as Abraham had loved him. Isaac was loved as a gift from God, as a blessing but also as a responsibility that must never be set aside. Now Isaac's son Jacob is following in his father's footsteps in seeking a bride from the land of his mother. Both parents wanted the right wife for him. Rebekah knew the area and the people. They had family there, so that would help, but it was still hard to see Jacob go. Releasing a child is hard because now they will have to step out on their own, but they must be released so that they can begin their own lives.

God knew that Jacob needed to spend time with him before going to the well, so he met him at Bethel. After Bethel, Jacob was ready to move forward

Genesis 28 tells the story of the encounter at the well. Jacob came to the well, and there were people standing around with their sheep. He learned that the practice was to wait for everyone to arrive, and then together they moved the stone. Then when they were finished, they moved the stone back into place. Jacob, anxious, no doubt, to find his relatives, asked about Laban, his mother's brother. Did they know him? Yes, they did. While they were talking, the beautiful Rachel appeared. She was approaching with the sheep. The others pointed her out to Jacob, and he immediately made himself known to her.

Jacob kissed her in a greeting. He kissed her as relatives did when they meet and "lifted his voice and wept." Many people, rabbis, priests, ministers, Sunday school scholars alike, have speculated about why Jacob did so. Some theologians felt that, on a spiritual level, he already felt that his relationship with Rachel would be loving but with many challenges. Jacob was a prophet, and while we see that very clearly at the end of his life (Genesis 49:1-2), even now we must wonder if he does not have some prophetic sense of the pain that lies ahead for the two of them.

Rachel was believed to be a teenager, perhaps fourteen (Hirsch and Seligsohn, 1906) at this time, and meeting her relative must have been something of a surprise. No doubt, she too knew the story of her aunt Rebekah who was found at the well and became the wife of Isaac. The others were willing to wait, as was their custom, for the rest of the shepherds, but here the story gets interesting.

We know that several men moved the stone together. Was this because the stone was too large for any one man to move easily? Was it because, over time, the community had learned to work together and they just waited and visited until everyone was there? Was Jacob showing some of his old impatience? Was he seeking to impress these new acquaintances? Was he, as many young men, when they are in the presence of beautiful young women, desirous of catching their eye and perhaps winning their affection? We don't know for sure.

When Jacob saw Rachel for the first time and learned who she was, he responded like many young people have down through the ages when they meet their first love. He was excited to see her and wanted to do something to let her know he was in the crowd. He wanted to be her center of attention as she was his. He was excited, happy, and apprehensive all at once. He rolled away the stone without any help so that Rachel could water her father's sheep. Things were going very well for someone who had just entered the community. Jacob must have breathed a sigh of relief, and, thanks to God, he had found his family.

Rachel rushed home to tell her father. Laban, in turn, went to meet Jacob. The men embraced in greeting. Laban kissed his nephew and then invited him home. This is, no doubt, what Jacob was hoping would happen. He had come to this country seeking his relatives, and he was warmly greeted and welcomed into their home. Did Jacob explain why he had left home? It is not stated. Even if he knew, Laban still welcomed him. He is, after all, family (Genesis 25:19–20). Like many close families, if someone is in need of a place to stay, they are welcome to stay as long as they like. It gives time to catch up on the family events, and it gives an opportunity to get to know this relative that they had never met. Laban said that Jacob was welcome to stay. He was able to spend time with his relatives.

Jacob had managed to be at the right place at the right time, and now his life was quickly changing.

CHAPTER 7

Winning the Hand of Rachel

> When Jacob saw Rachel the daughter of Laban, his mother's brother, and the sheep of Laban, his mother's brother, Jacob went near, and rolled the stone from the well's mouth, and watered the flock of Laban, his mother's brother. Jacob kissed Rachel, and lifted up his voice, and wept. (Genesis 29:10–11)

Jacob was entering into a new period in his life. He left home, in part because he had tricked his brother out of his birthright. At first hungry and faint, Esau didn't think much about giving up his birthright. After all, if he died of hunger, it wouldn't really matter (Genesis 25:32). Then when his elderly father wanted to give him a blessing reserved for the firstborn, Esau was honored and strove to find the venison his father requested. He prepared it so that his father would then bless him. Then his world came crashing down. Esau couldn't believe what was happening. It might have been one of those slow-motion moments when a person sees and hears what is going on around them, but it somehow seems like a dream or in his case a nightmare. It can't be real but it is real.

Esau was hurt. He was angry and, in that moment, wanted to take his brother's life (Genesis 27:41). Esau resolved in his heart to wait until the mourning period after his father's death was complete. No brother was better than the brother he had in Jacob. Home was now a dangerous place for Jacob to be. Esau was angry and understandably so. Isaac and Rebekah loved both Esau and Jacob and thought it best to send Jacob to Laban, his uncle, and other relatives. Away from home and family, he could do some growing up, some maturing, learn to think through the consequences of his actions before and not after the fact. There he could find a suitable wife and settle down. Jacob made the journey, encountering God for himself along the way. Knowing about God and hearing about God are both good experiences but neither takes the place of a personal experience with God. God spoke to Jacob, and just as importantly, Jacob listened and remembered the promises.

> Behold, Yahweh stood above it, and said, "I am Yahweh, the God of Abraham your father, and the God of Isaac. I will give the land you lie on to you and to your offspring. Your offspring will be as the dust of the earth, and you will spread abroad to the west, and to the east, and to the north, and

to the south. In you and in your offspring, all the families of the earth will be blessed. Behold, I am with you, and will keep you, wherever you go, and will bring you again into this land. For I will not leave you until I have done that which I have spoken of to you."

Jacob awakened out of his sleep, and he said, "Surely Yahweh is in this place, and I didn't know it." (Genesis 28:13–16)

Things were going smoothly for Jacob. He entered the city, quickly found a relative, and now was invited to his Uncle Laban's home. The first step had been taken, relatives, now friends, enter Laban's home, and Jacob is able to meet the relatives he had only heard about. Hospitality was and is very important in Eastern and Asian culture. Jacob was welcomed into the home. Laban was aware of his relatives in a distant country and, no doubt, wanted to know how they were doing. Like any family, this was probably a time of catching up and finding out those bits of information that bring joy to family members. During the first month (Genesis 29:14), there were probably many conversations.

It was clear that Jacob did not bring much with him by way of material possessions. While Jacob came from a family of means, Jacob did not appear to be a person of wealth himself. Was he robbed before arriving? Was this his opportunity to move away from the shadow of family and establish himself? The biblical narrative does not speak to these details. Initially, he volunteered to help, working for his Uncle Laban, helping him with his sheep. He was staying there with his uncle and wanted to help out. Laban could probably see Jacob's budding interest in Rachel. This first month gave Laban time to observe and make up his own mind about Jacob.

Jacob had been given directions regarding seeking a wife from his parents. His father was clear in telling him not to marry a Canaanite woman (Genesis 28:1). Rebekah went so far as to tell her husband, Isaac, that her life would not be worth living if her son married a Hittite woman (Genesis 27:46). His parents wanted Jacob to marry a righteous woman, one who would be a help to him and strengthen his own devotion to the true and living God. Neither of his parents wanted Jacob to marry a woman who worshiped false gods and idols that Canaanites and Hittites were known to worship. Both the Canaanites and Hittites were polytheistic, worshiping many gods, including some household gods and goddesses, Jacob would need to seek a wife elsewhere and where better than the land where Rebekah's family lived. Like many people, Rebekah's family may not have been perfect but she knew them and their way of life and felt that a suitable spouse could be found there. Just as she had come to love her husband's God and way of life the right wife would do the same for her son. During this season in biblical history, it not only was acceptable to marry a cousin but also was frequently encouraged. When one married within the culture, they could continue and strengthen their cultural bonds. Even today while many cultures would discourage marriage between close relatives, most recognize the link between marrying within the same cultural group and the continuation of the values and practices necessary for the cultural group to survive over time.

Living in the home of Laban, it was only natural that Jacob would consider Rachel as someone who would be a wonderful mate. Her beauty, her humble attitude in caring for the sheep, the respect he saw from others at the well for this daughter of Laban, and the bond that was developing between them was only the beginning of what would be a love story for the ages.

This matter of finding a wife was a matter that must have been in the back of his mind as he became comfortable in his new home. During this time, he came to know Rachel. Her beauty caught his attention when he first met her, but now living in the same home, he was able to learn more about her. He could observe her, talk to her, and learn her character. Like any young couple, this exposure to each other must have made a difference as they got to know each other.

The glances, the smiles, and the obvious affection that those in love hold for each other cannot be completely hidden. The initial connection might have been sexual attraction or infatuation, but as time goes on, the dimensions of love begin to develop, and what starts off as a tiny seed of interest begins to flourish until the hearts are filled with warm thoughts of each other.

After the first month, Laban decided it was time to discuss the future. He had observed Jacob's attitude and work ethic. Jacob had kindly helped out with the sheep, but now Laban decided it was time to arrange a formal agreement. This was the opportunity that Jacob wanted and needed. Jacob was quick to respond when asked about working for Laban. Was Laban surprised at Jacob's request? It is doubtful. As a cunning and perceptive man himself, Laban may well have observed and even felt the chemistry between Rebekah and Jacob. Was Jacob just another person who appreciated her kindness and beauty? Clearly, her personality created respect and admiration in the community, but in a traditional culture, any matches would be made by the parents.

Jacob's heart was out there for all to see. What of Rachel? Did she feel the same? Rachel's feelings are unspoken in the scripture. As with other women during this time in history, modesty was highly valued. Jacob might feel her interest, but it would be improper for her to openly express other than simple familial affection. The truth is we don't know how Rachel felt for sure at this stage, but her feelings become clearer later.

Jacob appears to have one focus, and that was the beautiful Rachel. What of Leah? Did Leah's eyes reveal her own heart? Was she too hoping for some sign, some indication that there might be even so much as a glimmer of affection? Completely smitten by his love for Rachel, it is unlikely Jacob would have noticed any interest on Leah's part. Jacob knew what he wanted. Oh, the singleness of purpose when true love invades the heart.

Jacob needed to impress Laban. He wanted to earn his keep. He could work with the family, but in fairness, Laban made it clear that he would not have his relative work for nothing. Did Laban have a plan even then? Jacob would be paid. Laban asked Jacob what he wanted in return for his labor. Jacob was specific. His mind and heart were clear when he spoked. Rachel, he only wanted Rachel.

This was a delicate matter. Without the resources of his family behind him, Jacob must work to earn her hand. When Abraham's servant sought a wife on Isaac's behalf, there was great wealth involved. Jacob was keenly aware of the events of his parents' marriage. He was now without family resources and financial support. He could not offer what had been given for his mother's hand. For a woman so precious and so deserving as Rachel, there is no doubt that Jacob would have offered it if he had it.

What would he have not given to gain the hand of his wonderful Rachel? With the Bethel experience behind him, he knew the right woman was critical to his life's journey. It was vital that Jacob not insult Laban with the wrong offer. To suggest that Laban's daughter was worth little might crush Jacob's dream of having her as his wife. He did not want to insult his host, his uncle, nor did he want Rachel to think that he felt her to be of little value. Jacob sincerely made an offer that he felt was appropriate for such a prize. Seven years, he offered. Seven years. Jacob would work seven years to earn Rachel's hand in marriage. Jacob might have held his breath a second waiting for a response, but to his satisfaction, the offer was acceptable.

It is important here that we take note of the fact that Jacob specified Rachel's hand, "Jacob loved Rachel. He said, 'I will serve you seven years for Rachel, your younger daughter'" (Genesis 29:18). Knowing his own pre-Bethel nature, Jacob probably knew that Laban was cunning and wanted to be careful. He wanted to be sure that his wording was precise and he couldn't be taken advantage of in this situation. Laban did not respond in kind, mentioning the name of the daughter who was to be given, "And Laban said, 'It is better that I give her to you, than that I should give her to another man. Stay with me'" (Genesis 29:19). Is he already planning to cheat Jacob? Laban, no doubt, remembered his sister Rebekah's experience and knew that Jacob came from means. Was he hoping for a similar dowry to that of Rachel? We do not have insight into Laban's thoughts, but clearly, Jacob has met his match in the cunning and deceptive Laban.

Hirsch and Seligsohn, in their study of this event, enrich the biblical text with rabbinical literature. In the very broadest sense, rabbinical literature can mean all of the rabbinic writing from throughout history. The rabbinic literature has historically expanded and enlarged upon the text. One might think of it as a source to further explain the primary text. Christians might think of it as a commentary source. Much of the rabbinical literature mentioned here reflects information from the Mishnah and the Talmud. Hirsch and Seligsohn suggest that just as Esau and Jacob were twins, their cousins Leah and Rachel were also twins. Was it assumed that the two cousins would marry at some point—the elder to the elder and the younger to the younger? If that was the case, Jacob's actions of deceit changed Esau's future blessings as the elder son. The effects of that decision would have an impact on the life of Jacob and his wives, with some questions forever unanswered. Jacob's grandfather has one wife, Sara. It was only at Sara's urging that Abraham father a child with her handmaiden. (This was a decision she later regretted.) Jacob's father had one wife: Rebekah This now becomes a very different path for Jacob, who becomes the husband of two women (Hirsch and Seligsohn, 1906).

Yes, it was permissible at the time, but as can be imagined, and as proven out by Jacob himself, there are inherent challenges in having multiple wives. This situation is magnified when the women are closely related.

In one of the most beautiful love stories imaginable, Jacob worked for seven years, but because of his great love for Rachel, it seemed like only a short time. What happened next might have been rejected as a Hollywood movie script as being too unbelievable. It was a wedding night to remember (or one might want to forget). It is at this point that we learn more about all involved in the unusual situation as well as have new questions introduced to which we have never received complete answers.

CHAPTER 8

Marriage

In the ancient world, marriage was a religious and social event that had no equal. Even birth and death, while important community events, could not compare with the beauty, the promise, the joy of two coming together to become one in the sight of God and man. Then, and to a very large degree today, the societal and cultural expectation was that people will marry. Even today, there is frequently some explanation given for failure to marry:

- "I focused on my career."
- "I helped to raise my sister's children."
- "I'm still waiting for the right person."

While many societies have come to tolerate, to a large degree, unmarried single adults, overall, outside a religious cloistered community singles, especially women, tend to be viewed with suspicion and skepticism. Marriage in the ancient world was very much the normative behavior and, to a large degree in most areas of the world, still is today.

Generally, it is assumed that a person will choose their own partner in the West, but even there, the tradition of asking for the hand of a woman from the father, for many, still exists. Traditionally, women lived with their parents until they were married. Even in today's society, many men still talk to the father out of respect before proposing to the woman. A number of countries, including India, Japan, Pakistan, China, South Korea, and Indonesia, still practice arranged marriages. In arranged marriages, parents select the spouse of their children.

The late Benazir Bhutto, the first democratically elected female leader of a Muslim country, was born into a political family with a great sense of service to their country of Pakistan. A bright and talented woman, she was educated at Oxford and Harvard. She made a difficult decision as a young single woman. In order to continue her work in Pakistan she would need not only to marry but also to marry in the traditional manner, an arranged marriage. Negotiations went on for over a year, and she met her future husband only a few days before the marriage. Bhutto is quoted as saying:

> I couldn't have a love match. I was under so much scrutiny. If my name had been linked with a man, it would have destroyed my political career. Actually, I had reconciled myself to a life without marriage or children for the sake of my career. So, keeping in mind that many people in Pakistan

> looked to me, I decided to make a personal
> sacrifice in what I thought would be, more or less,
> a loveless marriage, a marriage of convenience.
> The surprising part is that we are very close and
> that it's been a very good match. I'd love to arrange
> my own children's marriages. (IMDb.com, n.d)

Surprisingly, or maybe not so surprisingly, she was prepared to live in a loveless marriage, but that was not to be the case. In a truly fairy-tale turn of events, they became deeply in love. The marriage of Benazir Bhutto and Asif Ali Zardari ended only at the assassination of former Prime Minister Benazir Bhutto in 2007. While Bhutto's marriage was arranged by female relatives, it was the custom and tradition in Hebrew culture that the arrangements be made by the male head of the family. Arranged marriages, as well as those where individuals choose their own partners, may be successful or unsuccessful unions, depending on the couple involved.

Jacob appropriately asked the father, the head of the household, for Rachel as his bride and then for the next seven years worked to earn the hand of his beloved. The union would probably have taken place as a traditional marriage. From what we know about Hebrew and Arabic weddings of the time we know that marriages generally had several stages. The betrothal was first. This might be short or long. A two-year period might be considered a longer period, but Jacob' situation was different, and his betrothal was longer than might be expected. He was not coming with any family resources and had to work off his debt. This was something he was willing to do, really happy to do so that he could marry the woman he loved.

How did marriage and betrothal work? Jacob successfully completed the first expectation when Laban accepted his proposal to work seven years in exchange for Rachel's hand. The terms had been negotiated. This betrothal period was also a very real and binding commitment. It was much more so than our engagements of today. The betrothed parties were legally in the position of a married couple, and unfaithfulness was considered "adultery" (Deuteronomy 22:23). There was no bargaining, as is frequently noted in the East, but a simple agreement. Based on Laban's nature and tendency to be a man who could take advantage of situations, this was probably a choice on his part. He already knew what he intended to do. This agreement was deceptive and was a huge mistake for Jacob. He should have made Laban clearly state the terms to avoid any misunderstanding. Jacob exercised too much trust in his uncle and found himself married to a bride not of his choosing.

During this time there was not the formal ceremony that we traditionally observe in weddings today. In the typical marriage, when the time came for the marriage, there was no signing of the license, but there was great celebration. Understanding the background of the traditional marriage at the time helps to explain why Laban was able to successfully complete the bride exchange. In the traditional marriage celebration, there was the wedding processional. This was traditionally at night and quite the experience for the community. Was it more romantic and colorful to have it at night? Was it because people worked during the day? Probably the latter. The bride's attendants have spent hours preparing the bride for this special day, and then they wait. There is ceremony, ritual, and the bride prepares herself for the transition to a married woman. She prepares for her future where life will revolve around the man who has chosen her as his wife. Traditionally, women are moving into the arms and life of a man where they will build a family and she will provide love, comfort, hopefully children, and a lifetime of commitment. While it directly involved two people, it is about much more. Marriage is very much about the coming together of family and friends. It is also about culture, faith, and a belief in tomorrow. A group of men, friends of the groom, go to the home of the bride. The men are greeted by the female bridal party, the bride and her attendants traditionally go to the home of the groom. This must have been a beautiful sight to behold.

The wedding feast was at the home of the groom. It was a wonderful celebration. We do know that Mary and Jesus came to such a feast in Cana, and it was there that Jesus performed his first miracle, turning the water into wine (John 2:1–11) In Jacob's case, we do not have all the details of this wedding, but we do know that these celebrations could go on for several days in some cases.

The Genesis account of Jacob's wedding provide some detail of the marriage, which may have varied somewhat from the typical event. When Jacob completed his years of work, he went to his uncle and requested his bride: "And Jacob said unto Laban, Give me my wife, for my days are fulfilled, that I may go in unto her" (Genesis 29:21). Laban agreed and planned the marriage.

From the biblical account, we know that Laban gave a feast for the male guests to celebrate the marriage (Genesis 29:22). Laban was able to control the situation. This was necessary since Laban was planning a wife switch for Jacob. After a night of celebrating and drinking wine, perhaps Laban thought this might make the switch less noticeable, and apparently, he was right.

Around midnight, the celebration would have probably ended, and the couple began their new life together, enjoying the intimacy of their new marriage in private. Perhaps it was this time when Laban would have brought the bride to her new husband, the bride Jacob was both looking forward to seeing and, at the same time, the bride he was not expecting. Many people ask the obvious question, why didn't Jacob recognize Leah their first night together?

Over the years, various rabbis have offered different possible reasons. Dr. Rabbi Zev Farber discusses some of these possibilities in his article "How Is It Possible That Jacob Mistakes Leah for Rachel?"

The most obvious is that Jacob could not see her clearly in the dark space. Some believe that the room was without candlelight. It was late, and the tent was dark, making identifying his bride difficult, especially since he was sure it was his beloved Rachel. Some teachings of the Torah suggested silence during the actual act. Jacob, some feel, might have been a man of extreme modesty, which might have resulted in silence during the entire night. All of this would have made identifying Leah more difficult. There is also the possibility that the bride was not present during the feast and it was a totally male gathering. If that is the case, it is quite likely that Laban would have shared the wine generously. Jacob might have been one of many whose sobriety was seriously challenged on their wedding night. Laban then could have presented the bride late into the evening after the celebration. There also remains the reality of arranged marriages. While Jacob was a member of the household and there was no doubt some contact between Rachel, Leah, and Jacob, the societal traditions and limits would have been respected. Modesty was highly valued, and affectionate physical contact forbidden. Then there is too the traditional dress of the bride, which might easily conceal the identity of Leah (Farber, n.d.).

There is much speculation about the two sisters. Why didn't Rachel warn Jacob? Keeping in mind that, in arranged marriages, the details are worked out by the family, it is quite possible that Laban never discussed the matters with his daughters until it was near the wedding date. If he chose to do so, he may have even told Leah that she was the chosen bride, and she might have gone into the marriage believing that she was the chosen bride. Since the elder sister was expected to marry first, Rachel might have simply accepted the events at face value.

Did Rachel and Jacob have some sign between them as many believe, to avoid any tricks by Laban? Why would she have given the sign to Leah and remain silent? This possibility might well represent the love between two sisters. Later, there would be competition for Jacob and jealousy, but early on, it is quite possible Rachel would not want her sister disgraced before the community. Regardless of the particulars, clearly, the sisters became aware of their father's intentions, and within the cultural setting of their day and time, they would have been obedient to Laban regardless of how they may have felt about what was happening. Laban's plan had succeeded, and after a week with his first wife and an opportunity for her to win his heart, Jacob would marry Rachel. He would work an additional seven years for Laban, who, like most tricksters, might feel he was at an advantage. Both of his daughters were married, and he had fourteen years of labor from Jacob. Looks can be deceiving when dealing with someone who has the blessing of God upon their life. Laban's greed will cost him in the long run, but for now, he could feel that his deception had made him a winner.

The next morning Jacob became fully aware of how he had been deceived.

CHAPTER 9

The Hope of Love

Like thousands of women each day of the week, Leah lay with a man she loved. We know from her words later that it was her desire that he could return that love. She speaks of it on the birth of her son: "For now my husband will love me" (Genesis 29:32b).

Oh, how she wanted him to love her. Not unlike thousands of women, happily married, single and longing to be married or just longing to have a way to maintain a hold on a man that could not be maintained otherwise, the birth of a child can and does change things forever. Leah, a woman of prayer, knows that God is in this plan, but still she longs to have not only purpose but also the affection and commitment of the man she loves.

Lying there in the tent in the dark night, her veils were removed. She faced fear and hope. Her father knew, her sister knew, and she knew that this was not what Jacob was expecting. She was not who he was expecting. Leah brought treasured gifts to her marriage bed, her innocence, her love, and her commitment.

Far too many women offer these gifts too quickly and carelessly, using them as bargaining tools. "If I don't give myself to him, he'll leave me." Desperation drives them to offer what God meant for a sacred relationship to someone who seeks to momentarily soothe his own desire, and like Leah, the next morning they are rejected. They have offered a sacred gift, only to have it thrown back in their face.

Once experienced, many men and women continue to offer themselves to those who neither love nor value them. It is here that the real tragedy begins as they pretend they don't care, it's " friends with benefits," as if the union of a man and a woman in the most imitate act possible counts for nothing except a few moments of carnal pleasure. Many say, "It is just sex." It is sex as recreation, sex as a commercial enterprise, sex as a bargaining tool, sex as something very sacred twisted by dark powers into something so much less than what it was meant to be. How sad for those involved.

Is this to suggest that sex outside of marriage is never between two people who love each other? Certainly not! A great error of many Christians is to tell people how terrible sex is and how psychologically damaged they will become if they don't wait until marriage. The truth is sex can be rewarding and fulfilling without that permanent bond, but the reality is there are reasons that God has preserved it for marriage.

Sex can create a sense of false intimacy. Feeling close may be one-sided or a beautiful moment that lacks the effective communication, mutual respect, shared values, commitment and trust that is essential for long-term relationships. Attraction is a component but can't be the only quality that holds two people together. Like it or not, lasting relationships tend to take time, work, and effort. A shortcut to instant intimacy through physical bonding may disguise problems in the relationship that might otherwise be quickly evident. What feels like a perfect match in one area may overshadow the obvious failings in other critical areas.

Love is a feeling, but it is also a choice. It is quite possible that Leah understood her feelings for Jacob and believed that somehow, despite how the marriage started, he would learn to love her or at least feel some affection toward her. While she clearly understood the purpose of marriage in the culture was to have children and provide a home for her husband and not about love, it would still be a wonderful gift. The most intimate act between a man and woman is a sacred and precious thing designed not only to create children but also to strengthen intimacy. She wanted to be loved.

What did Leah feel as she lay the next morning discovered, her own emotions exposed as well as her body? Like many women who gave themselves to the wrong person or at the wrong time or under the wrong conditions, she probably just cried secret tears. Did she ask, "God, why couldn't he love me? Why can't I be the first choice for once and not Rachel?" Sex can enhance a preexisting love, but it cannot, nor is it designed to, make someone love you. It was a hard lesson for Leah.

Did she hear her sister's name called during the night and pretend it was her own, or did it cut through her heart like a knife through flesh, knowing that while he lay in her arms, it was Rachel who owned his heart. How she wanted that heart to be hers. Did she think he would realize it was her who truly loved him and embraced her in spite of the deceit, or was she just a woman, like many others, who so badly wanted the love of this man or any man that she would risk everything to gain it? The writer does not reveal the inner thoughts of Leah or dwell at this point on her personal tragedy. The rejected bride must face the community, her new husband who may have despised her at this point, and Rachel, the woman from whom she could not tear his heart in one night of love.

Jacob was livid. He was far too insightful not to recognize at least three things.

1) Laban has clearly tricked him.
2) Leah went along with the deception.
3) Rachel gave him no warning of what was to come. He trusted them all and finds himself in a situation he feels is not of his making.

> In the morning, behold, it was Leah! He said to Laban, "What is this you have done to me? Didn't I serve with you for Rachel? Why then have you deceived me?" (Genesis 29:25).

He has been cheated. He asked for Rachel and received her sister. If Leah lied to him on his wedding night, how would that be different from his own actions?

> Jacob said to his father, "I am Esau, your firstborn. I have done what you asked me to do. Please arise, sit and eat of my venison, that your soul may bless me." (Genesis 27:19)

He could have put her away, formally divorce her but he chose not to do so. What would be the point? She was already the talk of the community as it was, and Laban was willing to negotiate a new agreement.

> Laban said, "It is not done so in our place, to give the younger before the firstborn. Fulfill the week of this one, and we will give you the other also for the service which you will serve with me for seven more years." Jacob did so, and fulfilled her week. He gave him Rachel his daughter as wife. (Genesis 29:26–28)

This brings us to Laban motives. He cunningly does not mention the custom until after the wedding night and then gives Rachel to him for his second bride but only after Leah has had a week for her own celebration, though it probably didn't feel like one.

Again, we have no way of knowing if Laban had planned this action all along or if he recognized the love of Leah for Jacob and sought not just to find her a husband but someone she truly loved as well.

Is it possible that there was an agreement that Esau would marry Leah and Jacob would marry Rachel? If Esau was already married at this time, where would that leave Leah?

Leah moves from being the less-attractive daughter to the less-loved wife when the marriage of Jacob and Rachel is consummated. Leah may have made a mistake; she took a chance, and it didn't work out as she may have hoped. It was a chance over which she exercised little if any control, but her heart must have still longed for the miracle.

"The miracle," either expressed or unexpressed, is that the person she wanted and loved would see her and love her. The miracle is that her secret fantasies of lingering looks, soft touches, a life filled with love, children and children's children, and finally thinning gray hairs, faded eyes, and wrinkled and well-worn hands that still found their way to each other in affection would come to pass. The eyes she longs to see are those that even when everything else seems out of focus somehow managed never to lose sight of the beloved. Each glance is like the first glance.

It is the miracle that causes elderly men who might shuffle their feet unable to make the strong and steady steps of youth but still manage to move swiftly to open doors and give soft, caring touches to women who appear to be just grandmothers and great-grandmothers to everyone else but are still the object of their lover's affection and the center of their lives. It is the miracle that caused one man to make arrangements for flowers to be sent to his wife on a regular basis after his death (Regan, 2015). It is the kind of love that cannot stop an elderly woman from visiting her husband who may or may not recognize her. It is the miracle that drives men and women to be loving and faithful regardless of mental or physical health or economic situation.

It is what pushes and drives Leah to be a good wife, a faithful wife, and in the end, it is what may have won a measure of respect from her husband as well as a measure of love. She was not the beautiful Rachel, but she was Leah, who had her own kind of beauty. It was not as quickly evidenced as her sister's but just as real and just as precious.

Leah has strength, devotion, and a capacity to love that would have been a blessing to any marriage. History remembers her as the less loved but must also acknowledge that in her womb was nurtured Judah, the line from which the Savior came. God placed these qualities in her and knew that they would be a blessing to Jacob in time. Jacob loved the beautiful Rachel and remembers her even on his deathbed. She was the great passionate love of his life. Her death was one from which he never fully recovered, but it was Leah who brought him comfort in his later years and with whom he rested in death. God permitted the deception and allowed her suffering as the less loved but never forgot her. Leah cried out to God, and he heard her and blessed her with many sons, the sons she hoped would bring her love from her husband. As in the beginning, so it was in the end, Jacob and Leah.

CHAPTER 10

Complicity

Over the centuries, there have been endless discussions regarding Jacob and the first wedding night. Why did he not know the woman in the bridal bed was not Rachel? There are no clear-cut answers, but some interesting possibilities do present themselves.

Jacob cared for Laban's animals. He had to have a keen eye for such work but on the occasion of his wedding to the woman he loved he was probably so happy, so elated, that finally the day he had hoped for, worked for, and probably dreamed about had arrived that he may not have been very observant. He may have been relaxed, never considering the possibility that his bride was not Rachel. Why would he have any reason to doubt?

The heavily veiled bride and her attendants may have been brought to the wedding feast together. The attendants would have been loyal to Laban and his family. Families, especially families of means, have always valued loyal servants. These servants are sometimes seen as extensions of the family unit and, when well treated, tend to protect rather than harm their employers. If the attendants were present and aware, they had no reason to betray the secret. Under the circumstances, there is little doubt that Laban made sure the wine flowed freely during the meal. The last thing he wanted was for questions to be raised. It is late and well into the night or early morning when the couple found themselves alone. The deceit could have easily been carried out, but other possibilities have also been mentioned by various authors.

First, we must consider the nature of Laban. It is doubtful that Jacob could have lived for seven years in the household and not come to know something of his character. The irony is that Laban actions parallel some of the early attitudes and actions of Jacob.

Jacob was a trickster and knew how to use situations to his benefit. His carefully planned and executed plan to steal his brother's birthright leaves no doubt about Jacob's ability to practice deception. If, in fact, he did come to know something of Laban's character, would he have absolute trust that Laban would be true to the agreement? How much did Jacob know and when did he know it?

In the society in which they both lived, what would it have meant to a woman to be "left at the altar"? It is humiliating and painful today, but how much more so it would have been for Leah? Could it be that Rachel was unwilling to have her only sister held up for humiliation and public ridicule? If there was any love between the sisters,

Rachel would never have wanted that to happen. Her heart might have been broken, but she would not want the pain amplified by such a tragic and public treatment of Leah.

Might she have somehow had "shown her face." Just a glance would tell Jacob all he needed to know, but again, any tip-off to Jacob could result in great disgrace for Leah. Did Laban secure the sisters' cooperation by assuring them that Jacob would certainly continue to work for the second bride? Did he point out advantages to the two of them having the same husband, a good husband who would provide for them both? These things we do not know.

Laban's plan had succeeded, and after a week with his first wife and an opportunity for her to win his heart, Jacob would marry Rachel. He would work an additional seven years for Laban, who, like most trickers, might feel he was an advantage, both daughters married and fourteen years of labor from Jacob. Looks can be deceiving when dealing with someone who has the blessing of God upon their life. Laban's greed would cost him in the long run, but for now, he could feel that his deception has made him a winner.

Some individuals, apparently forgetting the culture of the day, tend to be very critical of Leah's action in going along with Laban's deceit. As his daughter, Leah was totally under her father's direction and control. It is doubtful that she would have even had a fleeting thought of "standing up to her father." In a traditional home, even today, a child brought up to love and respect their parents would have problems making such a choice.

If she had attempted to do so, we could only imagine her fate. Would she suffer physical punishment for her disobedience? Would she be dismissed from the household and left on her own? If that happened, could she even expect to find a husband in a society where family was extremely important? Who would shelter and take care of her? How would she regain her dignity? There was no positive choice, and most women of that age and many even today would not want to move in direct disobedience and defiance of their father. Leah obeyed the direction of her father. Did she do so willingly, or was she forced?

In the time Jacob spent in the household, it is clear who he loved, but is it possible that the two sisters, possibly twins, could have loved the same man? There is certainly reason to believe that Leah desired to have Jacob as a husband. If that was the case, she might have easily gone along with the idea, hoping that Jacob would come to love her.

Even more interesting than the motive was Jacob's reaction. It shows that there had been a real change in his character. His behavior shows compassion for Leah and her situation. Even in his anger at her, he did not refuse her intimacy (Genesis 29:31–32). We know this to be the case because God opened her womb. When Jacob discovers the deceit, he could have immediately dismissed and put away or remained legally married while totally ignoring her, but he did not. In fact, he immediately went to the person who he knew had put this plan together, Laban.

Laban reacted as a good trickster would. There was an explanation and an easy remedy that benefited Laban. Laban was following the well-known and established custom of the region. The custom was that the older daughter must marry first. That being the case, Laban provided his older daughter. Of course Laban didn't mention the custom until the day after Jacob's marriage to Leah, and only when Jacob approached him. Laban was accommodating, even willing to allow Jacob to work longer to earn the hand of Rachael. It was a simple matter that could quickly be resolved... to Laban's advantage. His Uncle could see the blessing on Jacob's life, and as long as Jacob stayed in Laban's household, Laban would also be blessed. If it took deceit to keep him there, so be it.

Jacob then did what Laban knew he would do. He agreed to work for Rachel. He would be married to Rachel after a week of marriage to Leah, and then he would finally have the woman he so desired. Did his heart allow him any choice? Of course, he went along with the agreement. This was an unusual agreement, but even Laban knew that you can only push a man so far. This way, everyone could save face. Laban got the additional work contract, Leah was not disgraced, and Rachel and Jacob could finally get married. One week more and finally his precious Rachel would be his forever.

Was Laban a father who was concerned he might not be able to "unload" the older sister? Did he really love his daughters and just use unscrupulous means to make sure they were married to a good man and no longer his responsibility? Either is possible, even both. But the request of a week with Leah would suggest he did want Leah to have an opportunity to begin a relationship. He did want her to be happy in her marriage. Regardless of who knew what and when, the marriage to Leah changed her life and sealed her destiny.

CHAPTER 11

Love Like Leah

Leah is many things. She is a daughter, sister, wife, mother, matriarch, and for many of us, she is a teacher. We can learn by listening to her and learning from her life. Leah teaches women of every generation about patience and faithfulness. Leah teaches us how to love and urges us by her example to be willing to take risks in love, to love completely, and to love without regrets. Leah cherishes love in this life but also holds tightly to the promises of God. Leah's humanity, as does ours, means that we will, upon occasion and despite our best intentions, make poor judgements, mistakes. We may act in ways that are inconsistent with our best selves or with the will of the Lord. Being human is what we are meant to be.

The ability to make choices is what gives us the free will to choose to serve God and humanity. The ability to make choices means we can turn away from the vain promises of the enemy that, like a beautiful well-worn path, quietly calls out. It calls us to a path of self-destruction and, all too frequently, shame, humiliation, and disappointment. With that free will, it is inevitable that individuals will not always make the wisest choices. This is anticipated and provided for as our Lord is able to turn the results of our bad decision-making into an object lesson so that we can learn, teach others from our behavior or decisions, and grow. We can adjust and grow. We can learn and grow. We can grow and change. We can change and be better tomorrow than we were yesterday.

We see some of Leah's evolution through the birth of her children.

> Leah conceived, and bore a son, and she named him Reuben. For she said, "Because Yahweh has looked at my affliction; for now my husband will love me." She conceived again, and bore a son, and said, "Because Yahweh has heard that I am hated, he has therefore given me this son also." She named him Simeon. She conceived again, and bore a son. She said, "Now this time my husband will be joined to me, because I have borne him three sons." Therefore his name was called Levi. She conceived again, and bore a son. She said, "This time I will praise Yahweh." Therefore she named him Judah. Then she stopped bearing. (Genesis 29:32–35)

While initially Leah holds on to hope that the birth of treasured sons will bring love to her marriage, something happens when Levi is born. She praises God for his birth in a way she had not done with her previous children. Initially, she hoped that the birth of her children would bring her closer to her husband, that he would love her for the sons she gave him, but now she didn't look to her husband. She wanted him to love her, but now she looked to God and praised him for his kindness and the gift of her son.

The ability to praise God is a gift, a gift that will encourage and strengthen, a gift that helps his people to see the blessings in spite of everything that might seem discouraging. It may be that the praise that flows from the lips, actualizes in the atmosphere of faith. Those words will wash over the brokenness of a spirit that is without strength, filling in the crevasses and breaks with the power of healing and the power of the Holy Spirit. Speak the words of life. Those healing words of praise may come from the lips, and as the words touch the hearing mechanism in the ear, as the message is carried to the brain, the memory of passed blessings are awakened, and that memory touches the faith component in the heart and the heart that felt no joy begins to rejoice. A heart that feels lifeless and dead will come alive because as the Lord begins to move, something starts to happen. People have been known to lift their hands and praise God even as tears streamed down their face, as loved ones departed this life, as dreams collapsed because the spirit of God speaks to the mind, saying, *I am changing things in your favor. I am moving in ways you have not seen. I am turning this matter around.*

Understand that each person has a role in their own turnaround. While the typical person may be most comfortable in a love situation that is transactional—you do for me, and I do for you—clearly, it may not always work out that way. In Leah's marriage, it took time for the relationship to develop and mature. When it did, it did not look exactly like the relationship Jacob had with Rachel. Marriages, good marriages, will not all look or function alike, but they will all be governed by love and acceptance, with either party giving the additional where it is needed on the non-fifty-fifty days. Leah may have desired the relationship that Rachel had with Jacob, but her marriage was different. It took a long time to develop trust, for the sisters to reconnect on the level where there was less competition and more working together for the good of the family. It took a long time to build a relationship that was truly hers, not based on trying to compete with her sister. Leah's marriage was different from her sister's marriage, but it was her marriage. Leah learned to accept the uniqueness of her marriage and gave her husband the love he needed from her. He learned to accept Leah in her own right, to see her loyalty, her faithfulness, her love for him.

God is gracious. Many have made terrible mistakes in the past, but it is a past God chooses to forget. What a paradox, that the God of all creation allows us to learn from the past and offers us not only forgiveness but also the gift of tossing that which needs to be forgotten into that wonderful sea of forgetfulness. We are instructed by our past, but our future is not controlled by it. Forgiveness is neither weakness nor capitulation. A person can love someone who is addicted to drugs or alcohol by giving them the support and direction that is needed, without giving them means to support their addiction. The love is unconditional and forgiving. The behavior must be shaped by what is needed in the situation. What is needed varies widely, within marriages, within friendship, and even between parent and child. Some people have been known to take their juvenile child to the police station and stand by them as the child gives accountability for a crime committed. Was this an act of anger? Actually, it was an act of love. Sometimes love requires tough decisions and painful follow-through. Leah's love was strong enough to stand the challenges of the marriage, and her faith in God grew and matured as she sought His comfort, as she learned to praise Him from a sincere heart.

As a person praises, they are able to release the negative emotions that are toxic to their mind and body. To carry anger, resentment, and hatred, day after day and week after week, eats away at the quality of life as well as the physical health. Ask God for the power to forgive. Forgiveness is no sign of weakness but a sign of strength. What greater example of the power of forgiveness than Christ on the cross—his forgiveness, his ability to love opened the doors of heaven to a criminal who hung beside him. Ask God for the ability to release the pains and wounds of the past. Ask for help to forgive those who it seems impossible to forgive.

This trial, this temptation to hate, may not be about them. It may well be about the person whose life is consumed with hatred and resentment, sometimes to the point that they don't want to hear the offending person's name or see their face. Trust God. Turn it over to him, over and over if necessary. Let it go. If you had the power to change them, you would have done so. God will deal with the individual who caused you pain, but he does not want that hatred to consume your life

Learn to praise. The praise can be a reflection of joy, when everything goes right, or it can be an acknowledgement that even on the worst day that can be imagined that God is still God, that he loves his creation, and regardless of what is seen at that moment, he is good. He is kind and he is working on behalf of his people. His people praise him for the blessings that have been given, the love that has been shared and, in the case of Leah, the beautiful children she carried in her own body and brought into the world. God is not only praised for what he gives but for who he is. He is righteous, powerful, loving, and he is the God of his people, always. If the situation does not change, he will change us so that we can endure. He will move according to his will so that the destiny he has spoken and preordained will be accomplished. His name will be praised and the glory is the Lord's. Within her spirit, Leah understood that she was blessed. Her life was not perfect, but she was blessed, and she had to thank God for those blessings!

> When Leah saw that she had finished bearing, she
> took Zilpah, her servant, and gave her to Jacob
> as a wife. Zilpah, Leah's servant, bore Jacob a
> son. Leah said, "How fortunate!" She named him
> Gad. Zilpah, Leah's servant, bore Jacob a second
> son. Leah said, "Happy am I, for the daughters will
> call me happy." She named him Asher. (Genesis
> 30:9–13)

Leah could no longer have children, but as was the custom during the time, she sent her maid to her husband to have a child for their marriage.

> God listened to Leah, and she conceived, and bore
> Jacob a fifth son. Leah said, "God has given me my
> hire, because I gave my servant to my husband."
> She named him Issachar. Leah conceived again,
> and bore a sixth son to Jacob. Leah said, "God has
> endowed me with a good dowry. Now my husband
> will live with me, because I have borne him six
> sons." She named him Zebulun. Afterwards, she
> bore a daughter, and named her Dinah. (Genesis
> 30:17–21)

The feeling of desperation seems to have passed. She still loves and desires her husband, but she also understands that God has greatly favored her. At the end of their lives, as it was in the beginning, there was Jacob and Leah. They did indeed dwell together. Leah learned to accept his passion and love for Rachel, but she also found her place in her husband's heart. Sometimes, it is more about the journey than it is about the destination. We need not continue to make the same mistakes. There may be consequences that follow, but that natural order of things does not bind us to the "original sin," or the original error in judgment. We can move on, and God will provide a future that is consistent with all his promises and all the love that he has given us. To be loved is a precious gift, to know that we are loved is next, and to respond appropriately to that love is our greatest act of wisdom.

Leah was simultaneously an obedient daughter and a risk-taker with more courage than the typical woman of her day or any period. As a daughter, she did as her father asked of her, knowing that the consequences could cost her the marriage and possibly any hope of love from Jacob. The natural order of the society was for girls to marry, become wives and mothers, and thus fulfill their purpose in life. To be an unmarried adult woman was an undesirable status. To have been touched by a man (willingly or forced) and then rejected by your husband also carried a serious stigma as well.

A wealth of emotions surged through Leah's mind and body. She risked so much for the possibility that her husband might come to love her. God saw her and was merciful and opened her womb that she might be fruitful, that her husband might come to love her for the children she gave him. It is important to note that her conduct and behavior is not to be confused with women who desire a particular man as their husband and become caught up in a name-it-and-claim-it mentality that ends with embarrassment and confusion. In one case, a well-known evangelist told the story of a woman presenting herself to him at church where he was ministering. God told her she was to be a bride. There she was presenting herself to someone who didn't know her with news of which he had no knowledge. Some in the congregation found the story amusing, but I was filled with pain and hurt for the woman. Sadly, hers is not an isolated event. The story has repeated itself many times over. In Leah's case, her actions were influenced by her father and facilitated in part by her sister (out of obedience to her father or a desire to keep her sister from being discarded, we are not certain), but Leah's actions were driven by a simple desire, please her father, to secure the affections of a particular man and fulfill her role in Jewish history

Each person has a longing in their heart that gives them hope, strength to keep moving forward. It is that longing that helps us to stand when we feel like falling. It is that longing, that destiny we must achieve, that pushes us to pay the price for our desired goal. Some have accurately observed that while salvation is free, there is a price to keep it. There is a price of devotion and faithfulness. We must not only choose salvation, but we must also choose on a daily basis to live in a way that honors God. We must choose to pay the price for our desired goals.

Rarely is that which is most valuable, most meaningful, without cost. In fact, we can be assured that the more valuable the gift or goal, the higher the cost. On occasion, individuals have found items of great value at a yard sale or hidden in an attic, but most times, people get just what they can expect. Every person must at one time or another decide if they are willing to pay the price for what they desire in life.

God was unwilling to simply overlook sin in mankind, and a righteous God required that there be a price paid for our sins, the blood of the innocent lamb. God sent his son out of love for mankind. Sin could not go without consequence. Jesus came to pay the price for man's sins. In his own sacrifice, he shows us how to love fully and completely. It is how he loves us and how we should love the Lord in return. We are human beings and fallible. To love those around us, to love with an open heart is dangerous and can be hurtful, but the love that gives completely is the love that will reap completely. There are always risks involved in opening one's heart, but the individual must decide if the risks are worth the rewards. To love freely and completely guarantees some disappointment, some pain, but it is also evident of a heart that is open. That open heart must be guarded with wisdom but not hidden in fear. To love is to open oneself to the possibility of disappointment, but also to open oneself to the rewards of that open heart.

Leah loved while holding tightly to God's promises. She was a matriarch, and as such, she was a woman who sought God's direction in prayer. She prayed and God answered. When we love like Leah, we understand that we are not destined to relive every mistake of our pasts but can build a better tomorrow. It is to understand that God was in control all along and that he will work all things out in such a way that his good ends are achieved. To love with God's destiny in mind is to trust him with the today we see and the tomorrow we don't know or understand. To love like Leah is to continue to love and live and strive to fulfill the Lord's will even when it feels hopeless and pointless. To love like Leah is to understand who you are and be true to that destiny. It is to love like the Lord is in control because he is. His will and his promises will be fulfilled.

PART II

Tamar: Collateral Damage and Why Sin Is Rarely a Solo Event

CHAPTER 12

The Nature of Sin

It is impossible to discuss David, his wives, and children without discussing the impact of sin on their lives. What is sin and what is the powerful pull of a force universally agreed to be a negative in the lived experience of mankind? Sin by definition and nature is any prevailing thought, initiated act or deed that propels a person to do that which God has forbidden, or not do that which God has required.

> Everyone who sins also commits lawlessness. Sin is lawlessness. (1 John 3:4)
>
> Woe to you, scribes and Pharisees, hypocrites! For you tithe mint, dill, and cumin, and have left undone the weightier matters of the law: justice, mercy, and faith. But you ought to have done these, and not to have left the other undone. (Matthew 23:23)
>
> But I tell you that everyone who gazes at a woman to lust after her has committed adultery with her already in his heart. (Matthew 5:28)

Sin originates from the commitment of the once great but now cast out embodiment of rebellion, and the enemy of humanity. His names and presentations of himself are many, including Tempter (Matthew 4:3); the devil, Satan, and deceiver (Revelations 12:9); Lucifer, son of the dawn (Isaiah 14:12); angel of the abyss, Abaddon, Apollyon (Revelation 9:11); Beelzebub the prince of the demons (Matthew 12:24); prince of the power of the air, the spirit that is now at work in the sons of disobedience (Ephesians 2:2); and the father of lies (John 8:44).

Evil exists because of a decision to take control. It is a failure to fully trust God's infinite knowledge and care. Ultimate wisdom is submitting to the control of God through Jesus Christ. Sin is ultimately about choosing not to submit to God. Hereditary sin or original sin as it is known by many, comes as a result of our own humanity. We are descendants of Adam and Eve, and their choice continues to be our inherited nature. Voluntary sin is a choice. It is those decisions of an individual that move them to choose their own path and knowledge over God's direction and purpose. Hereditary or original sin is the result of Adam's decision to share in Eve's rebellion.

It is easy to become that inexperienced driver who sees the keys on the table, available and unsupervised, and makes an instant decision. No insurance, no license, no problem. How hard can driving a car be and besides the car will only be borrowed for a few minutes. A bad decision is made. The not ready for prime-time driver grabs the keys and takes the car out for a spin and sadly all too often, an accident or near miss occurs. Rebellion and perceived self-interest are at the root. Self-interest is not inherently bad, but when it stands in opposition to God it consistently results in a greater consequence than first thought. The decision to accept Jesus Christ could certainly be defined as being in self-interest and is a blessing. But the voluntary choice to move in ways that are in variance with what God required or has forbidden constitutes not only bad judgment but active sinful activity.

In its biblical description of sin, *The Catholic Encyclopedia* notes:

> In the Old Testament sin is set forth as an act of disobedience (Genesis 2:16–17; 3:11; Isaiah 1:2–4; Jeremiah 2:32); as an insult to God (Numbers 27:14); as something detested and punished by God (Genesis 3:14–19; Genesis 4:9–16); as injurious to the sinner (Tob., xii, 10); to be expiated by penance (Ps. 1, 19). In the New Testament it is clearly taught in St. Paul that sin is a transgression of the law (Romans 2:23 ; 5:12–20); a servitude from which we are liberated by grace (Romans 6:16–18); a disobedience (Hebrews 2:2) punished by God (Hebrews 10:26–31). St. John describes sin as an offence to God, a disorder of the will (John 12:43), an iniquity (1 John 3:4–10). Christ in many of His utterances teaches the nature and extent of sin. He came to promulgate a new law more perfect than the

old, which would extend to the ordering not only of external but also of internal acts to a degree unknown before, and, in His Sermon on the Mount, he condemns as sinful many acts which were judged honest and righteous by the doctors and teachers of the Old Law. He denounces in a special manner hypocrisy and scandal, infidelity and the sin against the Holy Ghost. In particular He teaches that sins come from the heart (Matthew 15:19–20). (*Sin—Encyclopedia Volume—Catholic Encyclopedia*, n.d.).

The Bible has much to say about sin and how easily man can fall into the pattern of sin. *Voluntary act* are keywords when we think of transgressions and how it affects mankind. It is that thought of making a conscious choice that motivated lawmakers to distinguish between crimes that are committed by a sane person (capable of making a decision) and persons who are insane, even temporarily, rendering them incapable of exercising the mental faculties necessary to make a rational decision. While all mankind feels the impact of original or hereditary sin from Adam, it is the voluntary sin on which rests the major focus of this discussion. Through grace God has made provisions for hereditary sin that is experienced by all mankind. Freedom from the penalty of that sin is available to each person who chooses to become a member of the family of God through Jesus Christ.

While venial sins may be considered a small, noncancerous tumor that can either be quickly taken care of or allowed to grow and become more serious, mortal sin, in contrast, might be seen as a fully developed malignant growth. Murder, rape and other acts of violence and harm would come into the moral sin category. There are divisions and subdivisions in the discussion of what sin is, but regardless of all that, sin remains a violation of God's order.

God does not cause sin as we think of either venial or mortal sin but does permit humans the gift of choice. Which for some means that they will choose evil and sin over obedience to the true and the living God. There will be consequences that result from that decision, and they may have impact beyond the individual making the initial decision.

It is voluntary, the choice which is our focus. Sin promises a reward that satisfies human nature in some capacity—body, mind, spirit, social status, acceptance, or any number of other areas. The rewards fill a desire, and are temporary, the results can be unexpected, lingering, and more damaging than imagined, if imagined at all. The promises may be subtle and seductive. It might be a high, for instance, that has not been experienced before. For a few minutes of carnal pleasure, a nation of drug users has emerged in America. Many, now are incapable of living a typical life of work and family. Their entire being is focused on the acquisition and consumption of illegal substances.

Sin is seductive, and before it emerges as full-blown behaviors, it is frequently first incubated in the mind, nursed, fed and dismissed as only a thought, a harmless thought. The thought continues to visit and is entertained. It begins to seep from the imagined life into the outside world. It is not just imagined but can be real. The individual has the power and will to make it so. Like Eve, many don't see the end results until it is too late.

The idea of harmless sins is a popular notion, one that some use to justify their behaviors. "What is the harm they ask?" Some people explain their behavior to themselves, minimizing its impact, while they secretly continue to corrupt their minds, bodies, and souls. God brings balance and an understanding of the sacredness he has spoken into the world. Lack of balance changes everything. Instead of an appreciation of the sacredness of sex, for instance, its proper place in life and relationships, it is seen as existing solely for the fulfillment of individual personal pleasure. The focus shifts from God's purpose to human exploration and use. How can this act best serve me?

Sin is inherent in mankind and cannot be escaped. It is for this reason that God provides a remedy for sin. He allowed his Son to offer his life for us all. As for the original definition of sin expressed as a "prevailing thought," many would disagree. Thoughts are not sinful in and of themselves they may argue. The distinction is made for this reason. Scripture teaches us, "Blessed is a person who endures temptation, for when he has been approved, he will receive the crown of life, which the Lord promised to those who love him" (James 1:12). Temptation comes to every person, but the response is the decision one must make for themselves. Like the game show *Deal or No Deal*, a decision must be made. Will the thought be dismissed and a remembered scripture silently repeated? Will a simple look in another direction and a deliberate mental replacement, including gratitude for the blessings God has provided or perhaps a simple, "Lord, help today," will help the mind to refocus.

If every stray thought, even if not entertained, is seen as sinful, then does the possibility of pleasing God even exist? Being born into a world of sin is unavoidable but living a life of sin is the choice each person must make. Christ gave us an opportunity to choose forgiveness and restoration by his coming. It was the choice of David to allow his heart and mind to be led astray when he viewed Bathsheba. The decision was his. When he came to himself, he didn't blame God for allowing him to be tempted—he assumed responsibility for his own actions. Temptation comes and to be tempted is not sinful. It is human. It is the choice to entertain and linger with the thought of stealing from one's business, seducing one's neighbor, consuming substances that take away the ability to make rational and sane decisions that causes the problem. Avoid temptation when possible and, if necessary, respond as Joseph and get out of the situation by any means necessary. Temptation is not sin but yielding is a different matter.

New Boston Church in New Boston, Texas, included powerful insights in their sermon notes from a message on sin (Boston Church, 2014). The notes are detailed and highly recommended but for our purposes here we will focus on these three critical points:

1) Sin is real.
2) Sin requires something from you.
3) Sin rewards unexpectedly.

In the case of David, he was a man who truly loved God, but whose choices took him into the reality of hard truths brought on by sinful decisions. These truths proved to permanently impact his life and legacy. The reality of sin is just as true for every person. Choices matter and choices driven by the impact of sin can bring on painful and destructive results.

Sin always costs more than expected or the advertised price. The fine print tells the real story. There is guaranteed grief and sorry. It does not take long to realize that the product is less satisfying than it is promoted to be. A knock off designer item might seem to be the same as the original but close examination reveals the differences. Don't overpay for something that wasn't even worth the sale price and certainly not the full price you will now be charged.

It is easy to see the possible gratifying rewards of making decisions driven by negative forces but sometimes harder to imagine what the price actually is. Lies told to hurt someone else may be exposed, and the favor that was originally sought may now be lost as well as the respect of others, respect that was valued. Lies on a job application may go unnoticed for years, but then an individual who had worked hard to do well in a business may find themselves publicly dismissed for what seemed to be a small thing compared to all the good that has been done since being hired. Individuals who thought they were in a secret affair may find themselves drawn into a legal action and public exposure. In the process, they may lose the respect of others they cared about. Sometimes individuals are just forced to accept a hard truth. They have been used as a convenience, a tool, an item, something that was fun and entertaining but had no permanent place in the life of the assumed lover.

Sin is both expensive and painful. The rewards of sin do not begin to match the price that must be paid for it. Regardless of what is advertised, sin is always overpriced. It may be dressed in what appears to be a crystal ball gown, but it does not take long to realize it is just a paper dress in close proximity to a flame.

CHAPTER 13

The Family Tragedy

It feels like a Shakespearian tragedy, and in many ways, it may well be the spirit in which such tragedies are written. The most powerful dramas tend to be based on real life and this tragedy is one that grips the heart. The story of the House of David is recorded in the pages of scripture. These words give us hope, strength, and wisdom. They share the words that can save us from ourselves, give us insight into the past and hope for the future. It is to the words of scripture we turn for direction and where we learn more about ourselves.

Scripture confirms that it is our strength, our most notable gift or talent, that frequently opens the door to temptation and downfall. Sampson's strength is an example. To Sampson's credit, he came to himself at the end of his life, but so much was lost, so much good not done because of his personal choices. Even a beautiful angel who served God for a season became lifted up in pride and led a rebellion against God. It is easy to have a distorted view of reality when others see the gifts and talents God has given, and praise us. It is easy to think that it is really all about the created and not the Creator. It is easy to feel that the created is greater than the creator.

It is our nature, at its worst, to want to have power that was never meant for mankind. The power to control others, to command them, the power to take whatever we feel we want, the lust for power is as forceful as the lust for fulfillment of sexual desire. This is a fact to which Absalom can attest. The desire for power and control over others, to get everything we want, is within us all. It is our carnal nature that seeks to have us compete with God for Lordship. We cannot worship ourselves and our perceived power. We were made to worship God. Sadly, it is the carnal nature that when unchecked, unwashed by the blood of the lamb, that will take us not to the highest peak, but to the lowest depths of this life, a lesson David painfully learns.

David was a man with multiple wives, some of whom were probably, as per the time and place, more treaty and trophy wives than love matches. He could easily have continued to collect available women for his harem. Like all too many men and women, David saw a desirable person who was off limits, and he decided he would not respect boundaries. As frequently happens in matters of men and women, some blame Bathsheba for being a temptation to David. Why was she bathing when and where she was?

To suggest that the presence of temptation equals succumbing to temptation is to ignore personal choice, responsibility, and personal power. It is to succumb to the frequently repeated adage "You sin, I sin, we all sin. You can't help but sin." It is certainly possible that the residence of the ruler was higher than the others in the city so that he could look out over the city and he saw that which he did not need to see. It is also an insult to suggest that man is so depraved that one can only expect the lowest possible morality from each individual. It is to believe that there is no hope of a relationship of faithfulness and fidelity, no possibility that one man can respect the marriage of another man. It is to commit mankind to the impossibility of moral, ethical behavior and reduce man to being the pawn of the dark angel, incapable of approaching a God who requires what is not possible.

Even David didn't believe that to be true. Yes, man may sin, David sinned, but forgiveness must be sought. Inclusive in the forgiveness is a willingness of man to repent, to choose to submit to God's law, and to live as the Lord commands. Man is not perfect, and God makes provisions in his willingness to offer forgiveness. Still the elevation of personal desires above God's expectation is a step in the wrong direction.

When confronted by the prophet Nathan, David not only acknowledged his sin, but also repented and accepted the judgment of a holy God. He saw what his flesh desired. He heard the whispers of the one who made it look so easy, who had a predetermined plan to break off a low-hanging small branch and brush out the footprints in the dust so that no one would know he had passed that way. There is a miscalculation. There is always a ready plan that promises to conceal but in fact, is simply a postponement of the inevitable. The bookkeeper who cooks the books, abusers who hide behind computer screens, married lovers who meet in a distant city, a king who sends a good man in his service, to his death, they all felt the truth could be wrapped in a lie and no one would ever know. It would be kept secret. It was a miscalculation. The family tragedy is not that there was trouble in the House of David, all families face problems and trouble. The family tragedy is not that there was death of the young with promise. Sadly, many good people bury their beloved children who are the victims of disease, accidents, or even malicious acts. The family tragedy is how the House of David arrived at that destination, the place of unbearable sorrow. It is the story of the father who temporarily faltered in his responsibility to be true to God. It is the failure of a loving father who failed to properly guide, support and correct his children. The real tragedy is that, for a moment, he took his eyes off God, turned his ear to his faithful enemy, listened, and followed. David's actions reverberated throughout his family.

CHAPTER 14

David, It's Complicated

Is there a Sunday school youngster, past or present, who has not been thrilled by the story of the shepherd boy who took on a giant and won? As adults, many of us gain courage when we face problems and challenges that seem larger than life when we think back to David and God's intervention. David, the shepherd boy, David the warrior, David the writer of psalms, David the King, David the descendent of Ruth and founder of the House of David was extraordinary. He was a man of faith and love but also a man whose life was marred by sin and redeemed by God's grace.

An excavation directed by Avraham Biran, revealed the Tel Dan inscription, or "House of David" inscription, in 1993 (Staff, 2022). This was discovered at a site in northern Israel and was a fragment of basalt from the ninth century BC with House of David in Aramaic (King David [1040 -- c.970 BCE], c.d.). David ruled for forty years beginning approximately 1010 BC. He conquered land, and his skill as a warrior was legendary. We first meet the shepherd boy in First and Second Samuel. He is the least likely of Jesse's sons to be chosen.

The book of 1 Samuel records the moving story of the prophet's first meeting with the boy who would be king. God knew that Samuel's heart was with Saul during this season, but God let him know to just get over it. God had rejected Saul, and while Saul would continue as king for some time, the favor of the Lord was gone. Samuel was directed to go to Jesse the Bethlehemite. It was there the king would be found. He would be one of Jesse's sons.

> When they had come, he looked at Eliab, and said, "Surely Yahweh's anointed is before him."
>
> But Yahweh said to Samuel, "Don't look on his face, or on the height of his stature, because I have rejected him; for I don't see as man sees. For man looks at the outward appearance, but Yahweh looks at the heart."
>
> Then Jesse called Abinadab, and made him pass before Samuel. He said, "Yahweh has not chosen this one, either." Then Jesse made Shammah to pass by. He said, "Yahweh has not chosen this one, either." Jesse made seven of his sons to pass before Samuel. Samuel said to Jesse, "Yahweh has not chosen these." Samuel said to Jesse, "Are all your children here?"
>
> He said, "There remains yet the youngest. Behold, he is keeping the sheep." Samuel said to Jesse,

"Send and get him, for we will not sit down until he comes here."

He sent, and brought him in. Now he was ruddy, with a handsome face and good appearance. Yahweh said, "Arise! Anoint him, for this is he." Then Samuel took the horn of oil and anointed him in the middle of his brothers. Then Yahweh's Spirit came mightily on David from that day forward. So Samuel rose up and went to Ramah. (1 Samuel 16:6–13).

Saul was an imposing figure of a man. Physical presence and demeanor was one reason many of the people liked Saul. He looked like a king.

He had a son whose name was Saul, an impressive young man; and there was not among the children of Israel a more handsome person than he. From his shoulders and upward he was taller than any of the people. (1 Samuel 9:2)

David's brothers were similarly impressive. God made it clear to the prophet that what impressed people did not necessarily impress God. God looks on the heart. It is such a simple but essential lesson. It is an embarrassment to the church community that there are still churches where people are stared at and looked down on because of physical appearance, education level, dress, manner of speech, or other superficial concerns. We must value people as God values them. After being anointed, David just went back to his sheep. His destiny would unfold in God's time.

A talented young man whose music had a calming effect, he was summoned to play music for the king, and so he became closer to the inner circle. The Philistines were at war with the Israelites. Not surprisingly, the armies found themselves at a stalemate as they were on opposite sides of a valley. A visit to his brothers during the time of war further propelled David into his destiny. The Philistines had the upper hand with a giant who stood above every Israeli soldier. Fear was the order of the day. No one wanted to take on Goliath.

Now it became clearer why God sent Samuel to anoint David and not one of his brothers. God always saw the love, courage, and humility that were in the heart of the ruddy-cheeked young man. David took on the challenge. The traditional attire of a warrior was not needed because God had already prepared him. Sometimes it appears that the orientation and training that God takes everyone through is just unnecessary, a waste of time, but there is purpose in the path the Lord choses. David was more than a man whose music could calm the spirit; he had the heart and spirit of a soldier and a refined set of shepherding skills, especially when it came to the use of the sling. The time spent as a shepherd boy, taking care of sheep, protecting them, and caring for them had helped to shape his talent and courage. If a wild animal came to snatch up a lamb, there was no time to rush home and get help. He had to move quickly, his eyes had to be sharp, and his aim had to be accurate when he used stones as projectiles. Sensitive to the needs of those sheep, David was willing to do whatever was necessary to protect those who depended on him and guard their welfare.

Some of the same qualities that made David successful in caring for the flock were qualities that could later help him to be successful as he developed into a talented and well-loved leader of men. In animal husbandry, a person must hear and understand the audible and inaudible cry and concern of the animals who depend on the shepherd. This requires sensitivity to those who are served. David had to see, hear, and understand the sheep. With their keen sense of smell, sheep might respond to a threat that is yet unseen. David had to trust the natural strengths of the animals. He had to trust that because of their special gifting they might be reacting to something that is out of his sight and respond accordingly. With rectangular pupils, sheep have a very wide field of vision, around 270 to 320 degrees (Henriksen Garroway, 2022). They can see around them even when they appear to not be paying attention. They are very aware of what is happening. Sheep are natural prey for many animals, so they must keep watch. Even so they are still prey.

As a shepherd, David learned that God cares for even the weakest among us and all deserve protection. He took the time to understand them. Sheep are social, capable of a range of emotions, and not just dumb animals. Caring for sheep helped David to develop sensitivity, kindness, sharpen his powers of observation, and develop greater patience. David learned that, in the hour when he is needed, he must step forth, calm and accurate in his response. He must do what is best for the flock because he cares for them just as the Lord cares for us. In many ways, he used these natural talents but sometimes fell short when it came to his children.

When the Philistine looked around and saw David, he disdained him; for he was but a youth, and ruddy, and had a good-looking face.

> The Philistine said to David, "Am I a dog, that you come to me with sticks?" The Philistine cursed David by his gods. The Philistine said to David, "Come to me, and I will give your flesh to the birds of the sky and to the animals of the field." Then David said to the Philistine, "You come to me with a sword, with a spear, and with a javelin; but I come to you in the name of Yahweh of Armies, the God of the armies of Israel, whom you have defied. Today, Yahweh will deliver you into my hand. I will strike you and take your head from off you. I will give the dead bodies of the army of the Philistines today to the birds of the sky and to the wild animals of the earth, that all the earth may know that there is a God in Israel, and that all this assembly may know that Yahweh doesn't save with sword and spear; for the battle is Yahweh's, and he will give you into our hand." When the Philistine arose, and walked and came near to meet David,

David hurried and ran toward the army to meet the Philistine. David put his hand in his bag, took a stone and slung it, and struck the Philistine in his forehead. The stone sank into his forehead, and he fell on his face to the earth. So David prevailed over the Philistine with a sling and with a stone, and struck the Philistine and killed him; but there was no sword (in) David's hand. Then David ran, stood over the Philistine, took his sword, drew it out of its sheath, killed him, and cut off his head with it. When the Philistines saw that their champion was dead, they fled. The men of Israel and of Judah arose and shouted, and pursued the Philistines as far as Gai and to the gates of Ekron. The wounded of the Philistines fell down by the way to Shaaraim, even to Gath and to Ekron. (1 Samuel 17:42–52)

As David's profile began to rise, Saul's star was in decline. Jealousy ensued. With the help of his close friend and Saul's son, Jonathan, David managed to survive when Saul's jealousy broke out into a need to destroy the young man who never stopped loving and respecting King Saul. When Saul and his son Jonathan were killed in battle, David took men to recover their dishonored remains so that they might be buried with respect. David was a warrior who endeared himself to the people and to his soldiers. He was noble and understood what many leaders forget. He knew that the love of the people is more productive than the fear of the people. The lessons learned in caring for the sheep were not lost. This was a man after God's own heart.

King David's military prowess guided Israel from victory to victory. The kingdom was united and the House of David was established. Traditionally, kings would lead their armies off to war in the spring, but during this fateful year, David sent his men to fight but he remained at his palace. He goes onto the roof and happens to glance at a woman bathing. David was surrounded by beautiful women, but this woman caught his attention. He wanted to know more about who she was. David inquired and quickly found out that she was the wife of Uriah the Hittite, one of his soldiers.

The king sent for the woman, knowing she was someone's wife. The accidental glance evolved into a gaze. The gaze then stoked his curiosity and interest, fueling his own desires and emotions. David was moving in an unhealthy direction, but there was still time to change his mind. The woman was married to someone in his army, a loyal soldier. That marriage should have been respected. Sin rarely leaps onto our path full blown. In fact, if more people could clearly imagine the end destination, they might choose to abandon the path they have recklessly chosen. Many, probably most, who are caught in a web of sin like an insect hopelessly trying to escape find themselves in similar situations to David. They have been moving by degrees into behaviors that will cause them harm or grave regret or both.

When David meets Bathsheba in person his desire only heightens. The die is cast when the couple becomes intimate. Some people raise the obvious question, couldn't she just say no. Saying no to power, wealth, and influence, especially for a woman in a patriarchal society, just might be harder than it sounds. While it is not stated, refusing someone in David's position might have been more difficult than one might expect. We don't know how the woman felt about this meeting. We only know that the romantic encounter resulted in pregnancy for Bathsheba. The term *secret sin* is almost a misnomer. One can usually assume that what they most want to be kept secret will probably be exposed at some point. It is part of the deception of sin to believe that once entangled one can control and master sin, one can command it to stay hidden. Know that the sin will probably master, just as the web ensnares the insect.

When David's lover shares with him that she is pregnant with his child, David has a situation on his hands. The king does not want to be exposed. He needs a way to hide his secret. David came up with what should have been the perfect solution. King David sent for Uriah to come from the field of battle. The king said he wanted Uriah to have some time to refresh and spend time with his wife. A man of loyalty and integrity, Uriah did not want to spend downtime with his wife while his fellow soldiers were still on the battlefield, while they were sleeping in tents. Instead of spending the night with his wife, Uriah spends it with the palace servants. He refuses the comfort of his own bed and wife (II Samuel 11:6–13). Ironically, a soldier is showing more integrity and character than the leader of the army, the king.

David is now in total despair. He sends word to the leader of the military operations. Joab was told to send Uriah out front where the fighting was the fiercest and then to pull the other soldiers back so that Uriah was left alone. Uriah, the loyal soldier, was killed, and God himself took note of what had happened, the hidden sins. Uriah's wife went through the required mourning period, and then David married her. She bore her son, and all seemed to be going well, but their sin was not to remain hidden.

A chance view of a beautiful woman bathing, a pregnancy, and the murder of a faithful soldier and friend left a permanent mark on the life and legacy of a great man. As usual, in this case and many others, there was collateral damage. A good man died on the battlefield in an effort to try and cover up David's sin. The problem with secrets and cover-ups is that God never gets the memo. He brings truth and justice. While sometimes late to the party, truth never fails to show up and never fails to bring light into the darkest corner. Power and lust are a dangerous combination. The noble, daring David sinks into sin. When exposed by the prophet, he acknowledges his wrongdoing, humbles himself, seeks God, and accepts the consequences of his actions.

Sometimes people attempt to explain and, in some cases, justify what cannot be justified by asserting that "you can't help but sin." A nod to the universal heritage of original sin cannot be used to justify the power of individual choices. Each person does have the power to make choices in their own life. One cannot celebrate the results of positive choices while denying accountability for destructive ones. David acknowledged as much. There was a price to pay, the death of his unborn child and a sword that would remain in his house. Death and destruction became permanent members of the House of David.

CHAPTER 15

Amnon, Wicked Is as Wicked Does

Amnon was very much a son who needed the strength of a father to guide him. David was a chosen vessel, a king, a musician, and a warrior beloved by the people, but in some ways, he fell short in his critical responsibilities as a father. This happens all too often. It is difficult to find the right balance between ministry, life, and family and yet it must be done. Eli was a priest who loved God and served forty years, yet his children brought shame to the temple (Mindel, n.d.).

Eli, like David, was devoted to the Lord. It was Eli who mentored the young Samuel and taught him how to serve the Lord as a priest. Samuel became a spiritual giant, in part, because a great man of God mentored him. Unfortunately, Eli's own sons brought dishonor and disgrace upon him. Despite being warned about his children, Eli still found it difficult to correct them (I Samuel 2:13–17, 29–34). Hophni and Phinehas were immoral priests who stole from God and cheated the people, yet their father did not take action against them. Scripture describes the brothers in frank terms. "Now the sons of Eli were sons of Belial; they knew not the Lord" (I Samuel 2:12). Belial referred to the boys' wickedness. They were as wicked as their father was holy. God loved Eli but would not suffer the sins of his sons.

Perhaps Eli thought his sons would "grow up" and start doing the right thing. Eli, a good man, would not remove them even after the Lord sent a clear warning. Eli is not alone in this challenge. There are contemporary figures who allow their children to serve in positions in the ministry even after the parent realizes there are serious issues of responsibility or willingness to live a consistent, holy life. Perhaps they are hoping that their offspring will change. They ignore behavior that might be condemned or corrected in another. Some people find it difficult to exercise discipline with those closest to their heart, but God's expectations cannot be ignored or set aside. Amnon was the son of a king but also a young man who needed discipline and direction as do all young people. He had opened his heart to an ungodly spirit that now ruled his conscious thoughts and desires.

Parents must be especially aware of these spirits that behave like a computer virus. They attack the vulnerable, taking them to where they want their mind to be, focusing on thoughts that are neither healthy or fruitful. One way this happens is with pornography. Images that were viewed for pleasure imprint themselves upon the mind and now dominate the thought life. Parents must exercise accountability with minors and their access to sites and locations on the World Wide Web designed to destroy their innocence and capture their thought life.

As every parent, David meant well but could probably be considered an indulgent father when it came to the children he loved. This love is especially evident when he loses Absalom and the first baby he shared with Bathsheba. Neither loss was easy, and neither was without warning. He lost his infant child as a direct result of his own sinful choices in arranging the death of his lover's husband. The handsome and very much loved Absalom was another casualty of the prophetic word offered by Nathan. God forgave David, but his sins came with a price, "The sword would never depart from the House of David" (II Samuel 12:10). David didn't know who or when but he did know that there would be violence and death because of his sins. Parenting is no easy job for anyone, especially someone who is busy fighting enemies, building an empire, and sadly, in David's case, becoming entangled with another man's wife. A part of parenting, a very important part, is modeling the behavior that the parents want to see in the child. David sometimes failed in this regard, but David was always an example of a man who would humble himself before God and repent.

Sadly, Amnon followed his father's footsteps in some ways he should not have, and failed to follow them in the ways that might have saved his soul and life. Amnon was, for a season, first in line for the throne. As the oldest living son, he could look forward to ruling the kingdom his father was building. Apparently, Kileab, his older brother, had passed away or was unable to serve, and this meant that Amnon would do well to spend his time preparing for the task that would one day come to him. That did not appear to be his preoccupation. A bright future, honor, and prestige all unraveled because the prince allowed the enemy of his soul to snatch it all away. To rule a kingdom, a man would do well to learn how to manage his own life, a talent Amnon was lacking.

Amnon became obsessed with his half sister, a beautiful, charming woman who had a future of her own until her brother's deceit destroyed it. Many translations used the word love to describe his feelings.

> He said to him, "Why, son of the king, are you so sad from day to day? Won't you tell me?"
> Amnon said to him, "I love Tamar, my brother Absalom's sister." (II Samuel 13:4)

Love seems to fall short of the emotion that was driving Amnon. The physical and emotional factors that come together when a young person is maturing physically are powerful and can overtake reason and logic. It is the carnal man who wants what he wants when he wants it. This is why it is so important for human passions to be submitted to God and human behavior to be under the control of the individual. When there is no self-control, the passions can become unmanageable as the enemy takes the driver's seat. The song "Don't Let the Devil Ride" sums it up by reminding listeners that when they allow the devil to ride he will soon want to drive. "Don't," the songwriter encourages the listener, "Let him ride".

Without a moral compass, passions rule man instead of man ruling his passions. Out of the failure to be in control of one's own life and body comes adultery, incest, rape, sex trafficking, buying and selling people for what is said to be pleasure but in fact is only unbridled passions and drives controlled by the enemy of the soul. People are objects to be used and discarded. They exist to satisfy the desires and then just need to go away. The great talents of the enemy are deception and destruction. He says love but nothing about the above behaviors has any relationship to love. The scripture clearly defines what love looks like.

> Love is patient and is kind. Love doesn't envy. Love doesn't brag, is not proud, doesn't behave itself inappropriately, doesn't seek its own way, is not provoked, takes no account of evil; doesn't rejoice in unrighteousness, but rejoices with the truth; bears all things, believes all things, hopes all things, and endures all things. (1 Corinthians 13:4–7).

> Many waters can't quench love, neither can floods drown it. If a man would give all the wealth of his house for love, he would be utterly scorned. (Song of Solomon 8:7)

Love by nature puts the desires and needs of the beloved first. None of this describes the immature and undisciplined Amnon. The prince had only to ask his father for any woman in the kingdom. As his heir, David would view him favorably but as prophesied by Nathan there was disaster on the horizon. Amnon, like many others, wanted what he could not have. In his case it was his half-sister, Tamar. Her beauty caught his eye. He became totally focused on her and how he could possess her. His passion lacked the hallmarks of love, concern for her welfare, a desire to have a future with her. She was a conquest.

He dares not share his evil desires with everyone, but he felt comfortable sharing them with his cousin who immediately came up with a plan to get Tamar into Amnon's room. He needed, Jonadab expressed, only to share his need for Tamar to come and cook some food in his presence so he could eat it and feel better. Amnon was so totally overcome with passion that he had lost weight. The treacherous Jonadab knew what to do to help Amnon, and the plan was put into place. Before, he was simply wasting away in lust, but Jonadab, to his eternal disgrace, provided a plan. Having no idea what Amnon was planning, King David directed Tamar to do as Amnon requested. Everything was falling into place. She was finally there in his chamber, close enough to touch, to embrace. Amnon sends everyone out of the room, and Tamar, realizing what is happening, pleads for her life. The law made provisions for woman who are raped.

If there is a young lady who is a virgin pledged to be married to a husband, and a man finds her in the city, and lies with her, then you shall bring them both out to the gate of that city, and you shall stone them to death with stones; the lady, because she didn't cry, being in the city; and the man, because he has humbled his neighbor's wife. So you shall remove the evil from among you. But if the man finds the lady who is pledged to be married in the field, and the man forces her and lies with her, then only the man who lay with her shall die; but to the lady you shall do nothing. There is in the lady no sin worthy of death; for as when a man rises against his neighbor and kills him, even so is this matter; for he found her in the field, the pledged to be married lady cried, and there was no one to save her. If a man finds a lady who is a virgin, who is not pledged to be married, grabs her and lies with her, and they are found, then the man who lay with her shall give to the lady's father fifty shekels of silver. She shall be his wife, because he has humbled her. He may not put her away all his days. (Deuteronomy 22:23–29)

Did she cry out as required by law? If so, no one reported it, but then, who would stand against the king's oldest son? Who would dare challenge his word? One more lie would be nothing compared to what he had already done. Some people would say, she was there, she must have known what he had in mind. Then as now, some people blame abused and exploited women for their own suffering. Tamar trusted her half-brother, which was natural and expected. She obeyed her father, who sent her to him. She followed his directions and made food for her half-brother. Like thousands of others, she had done everything she knew to do that was right, and now the shame was unbearable.

> Then he called his servant who ministered to him, and said, "Now put this woman out from me, and bolt the door after her." (2 Samuel 13:17)

She begged Amnon not to rape her. What he did was neither natural nor reasonable. Her pleas to Amnon fell on deaf ears. After he rapes her, Amnon no longer wants to see or be in the presence of "this woman" and has her removed from his room.

His behavior sounds eerily like some contemporary crimes. A woman simply wanted to use a ride share but ended up with the wrong driver (CBS Interactive, 2021). Another woman completed giving an exam and caught a ride with someone she was familiar with from a previous meeting. She was raped, became depressed, and later took poison (*Hindustan Times*, 2021). Like Tamar, they were just living their lives, and the evil found them.

Indifferent to the fate of the now disgraced Tamar, Amnon, like most of us, failed to fully appreciate the extent of the fallout from his behavior. Sin has a way of making us feel like we are in control, but in fact, evil has taken the driver's seat. The abuse of his sister resulted in Amnon's own death. He was killed by Tamar's brother, Absalom. Amnon foolishly thought all was well between them after the sexual assault of Tamar, so when he was invited to a banquet given by their brother Absalom, he attended. He did not realize the banquet was just a ruse, an opportunity for Absalom to take revenge for the assault. Amnon was murdered at the banquet by Absalom's servants following Absalom's orders. The pursuit of sexual pleasure through the abuse of his half- sister cost Amnon his life. Amnon traded his life for a few minutes of pleasure. The sword has touched flesh, the first victim, the innocent baby of Bathsheba and David. The second was a virgin seeking to bring comfort to her "sick half-brother." The collateral damage of sin can be far reaching, and for David, it was just that.

CHAPTER 16

Jonadab, Blood Relative and Fake Friend

President Richard Nixon will forever be linked to Watergate. He was named as an unindicted co-conspirator because of his actions in covering up the Watergate burglary. A co- conspirator is someone who takes part in a conspiracy to commit a crime but who is not charged in the indictment. Their fingerprints are all over the situation, but somehow they manage to avoid the legal consequences.

And so the discussion turns to Jonadab. The expression "throw a stone and hide your hand" describes him perfectly. Were he around today, he might well be the corrupt, friendly college upperclassman, inviting freshman girls to the off-campus party. They are excited to have been invited to what sounds like a great fun time. It is only later that they realize they were set up to be victims. They were invited as the entertainment, to be drugged, sexually exploited, and discarded. Their reputations will be left in the dirt while their perceived friend continues to disrupt and destroy the lives of others. With no direct link to the crimes committed, he escapes legal accountability, but without his participation, the crimes may have never happened.

While Jonadab's name means "generous deed," his actions did not live up to his name. Under the guise of friendship, he gives advice that eventually ends in the rape of Tamar and the murder of Amnon, his purported friend. While filled with lust and desire for his half-sister, Amnon had no plan or ideas of how he could get her alone and carry out his lustful desires—until his cousin came up with a plan.

> But Amnon had a friend, whose name was Jonadab, the son of Shimeah, David's brother; and Jonadab was a very subtle man. He said to him, "Why, son of the king, are you so sad from day to day? Won't you tell me?" Amnon said to him, "I love Tamar, my brother Absalom's sister." Jonadab said to him, "Lay down on your bed, and pretend to be sick. When your father comes to see you, tell him, 'Please let my sister Tamar come and give me bread to eat, and prepare the food in my sight, that I may see it, and eat it from her hand.'" (II Samuel 13:3–5)

The evil in Amnon may well have remained the stuff of fantasies and lustful dreams except for the plan provided by Jonadab, an individual who is described in *The Message* Bible as "streetwise" and the *New International Version* as "shrewd" (II Samuel 13:3). While we don't know what was happening in Jonadab's mind, a reasonable person would be concerned for their cousin. They would have to consider the fact that someone who has been so possessed by evil that their fantasies have resulted in weight loss and an unshakable desire to commit a sin that might result in death according to the law is in real trouble and needs the prayers and good advice of a friend to save him.

At this moment when the unstable Amnon most needs the guiding hand of his father and the strength of a friend, both seem unavailable. Jonadab throws the man drowning in his own lustful dreams not a lifeline but an anchor to drag down not only him but also the innocent Tamar. While Jonadab is identified as a friend the question is, "Are these the actions of a friend?" Would a friend try to "snap Amnon out of this state of desire and delusion," or would he feed into his deteriorating mental condition. Was he aware that legally Amnon might be able to take Tamar as his wife and have what he desired?

A streetwise man living on the fringe of royalty could have easily found out the information, but he had other suggestions. The rock was already in his hand, evil already in the room, and a victim already selected. Friendship is dominated by concern, compassion, and understanding. Friends want the best for each other and celebrate with them when success comes their way. Amnon was in line to become king as the oldest son of David. Jonadab saw the privilege and power of the position but not the need for Amnon to be an example for the people.

Frequently, people will use family connections to their advantage. The crafty Jonadab surely knew how to use his relationship to King David, his uncle and his friend and cousin, Amnon. In addition to keeping his connections to David active for a season, after Amnon's death, he even backed Absalom in his rebellion. Jonadab's continued involvement in matters of the family and of state would suggest that neither David nor Absalom fully appreciated the fact that Jonadab represented a poisonous branch of the family and should have been cut off. The value of family connections and privilege appear to outweigh moral and ethical behavior for Jonadab.

Without the Lord, it is easy to become inwardly focused. It is easy to see oneself as the center of the universe with every action designed for personal amusement, satisfaction, benefit, or advancement. Such people must be avoided at all costs. They may flatter and charm, but relationships are ultimately defined in terms of personal benefit. Amnon desperately needs a friend at that moment, a friend who would speak the truth regardless of how it was received. Instead, he had Jonadab, the streetwise associate, the blood relative, and fake friend. The prophet spoke, and the sword glided through the air, taking victims. A rock is thrown and a hand hidden, as prophecy was fulfilled in the House of David.

CHAPTER 17

Absalom,
The Loss of Promise

There is beautiful, there is handsome, and then there was Absalom. Absalom was striking in appearance, a sight to behold. He was the perfect leading man for a Hollywood movie, only he needed no film edits or makeup. It was all natural.

> Now in all Israel there was no one to be so much praised as Absalom for his beauty. From the sole of his foot even to the crown of his head there was no defect in him. When he cut the hair of his head (now it was at every year's end that he cut it; because it was heavy on him, therefore he cut it); he weighed the hair of his head at two hundred shekels, after the king's weight. (II Samuel 14:25-26).

Absalom was the third son and his sister was Tamar. "Now these were the sons of David, who were born to him in Hebron: the firstborn, Amnon, of Ahinoam the Jezreelitess;

the second, Daniel, of Abigail the Carmelitess; the third, Absalom the son of Maacah the daughter of Talmai king of Geshur (1 Chronicles 3:1–2). Amnon was a half brother to both Tamar and Absalom. Tamar was taken in by Absalom after her traumatic experience. Her status as a beautiful princess with a promising future was now history and she just needed a place to live out her life. Her brother gave her shelter. He reported what happened to his father.

David's reaction was similar to that of Eli, the high priest, when he was confronted regarding his sons and their wicked behavior. He didn't like it, was angry, but did nothing to correct the obvious wrong.

> Tamar put ashes on her head and tore her garment of various colors that was on her; and she laid her hand on her head, and went her way, crying aloud as she went. Absalom her brother said to her, "Has Amnon your brother been with you? But now hold your peace, my sister. He is your brother. Don't take this thing to heart." So Tamar remained desolate in her brother Absalom's house. But when king David heard of all these things, he was very angry. (2 Samuel 13:19–21).

The penalty, if true, for such a sin was severe. For all his son's faults, David still loved all of his sons. There is no evidence that he did anything to confront Amnon about the behavior. There is no record that he sought to comfort his daughter and bring her into his own home at this time. David might have felt guilty about his own sin, and having heard the prophetic word from Nathan, he might have just accepted it as part of his punishment. This second step in the punishment was just beginning.

Absalom was both ambitious and talented. He was something else. He was a brother who loved his sister deeply, a wonderful trait. He was also a man capable of ruthless revenge. He quietly waited, but after two years, no action had been taken against the man who ruined his sister. The loss of virginity prior to marriage was a loss, a stain, with lifelong consequences. Marriage proposals were lost, unless the offender wanted to marry the woman in question.

After the rape, Amnon had no interest in Tamar. The experience was a scarlet letter of its own in ancient society. Even today the word *ruined* is frequently used to describe the situation in some societies. Who wants a ruined woman? Absalom's actions on behalf of his sister showed love, respect, and perhaps even a belief that his father might, "do the right thing," Absalom had his sister to hold her peace, and he reported to David what had happened and waited and waited. He saw what this had done to the bright light that was his sister who now walked in shame. She, as many others, might have experienced the impact of rape-related PTSD. The brother who loved her could see what the experience had done to her. He experienced pain and anger as he waited for some punishment for Amnon.

Where was her father? We don't know. It is a call and refrain that has become a regular beat in contemporary society. Many men don't understand that sometimes the

right words mean less than the physical presence. Nothing replaces the love and care of a father, especially when a child, male or female, is suffering. A father does not have to have all the answers, sometimes the answers mean less than the love that an embrace can communicate. "I will do my best" means more than lies and promises that cannot be kept. Sometimes silence and tears mean more than a thousand words. A father who is there can make all the difference to a daughter who needs to know that the man who help make her loves her if no other man appreciates her value.

A respected preacher in one small community reportedly lost his temper and laid "holy hands" on a man who was physically abusing his daughter. The story was said to have been reported in the local newspaper, and while some may have condemned the man—and surely, he had to ask God's forgiveness—I recall no one who spoke ill of him. Fathers understood, and women were quietly thankful. A daughter needs her father. If he is not there, who will teach her what a man should be and how a man should care for his family? Did David embrace his suffering daughter? There is no record to support some comfort from the man from which it would have meant so much. If David wanted this to go away so that his son might be spared, he would be disappointed.

Absalom carefully planned his revenge. Two years later, both Amnon and King David might have assumed that Absalom had forgiven the act committed against Tamar. Absalom had not shown any hostility toward his brother, and while David was cautious, he did not feel his oldest son and heir to the throne, Amnon, was in danger. Absalom, on the other hand, felt it was time for him to take action. His sheep shearers were at Baal Hazor, and Absalom invited his brothers to a sheep-shearing feast. Absalom also invited his father. David declined because he felt having so many people over might be something of a burden to Absalom. The prince then asks, almost as an afterthought, if Amnon could attend. This was the son David knew he needed to protect after his criminal act against Tamar. Amnon was next in line to the throne and needed to be protected. Amnon was one of the kings' sons and, no doubt, would be looking forward to fellowshipping with his brothers.

But still, David hesitated. He knew there was bad blood between Absalom and Amnon. Absalom, however, was persistent. Maybe David thought Absalom had forgiven his brother for his acts and forgiven the king himself for not taking action. Regardless, David agreed, and he lived to regret that decision.

The act of Absalom inviting his father, knowing what he had in mind, is chilling. It was grace that kept David from being there and possibly seeing his son struck down. It would have been an act of unusual cruelty on the part of Absalom. His anger had become toxic and dangerous. Before the banquet, Absalom instructed his servant to kill Amnon. As Amnon became relaxed with the wine and was enjoying himself, his death came quickly. Absalom was not only not surprised but expecting the murder when it happened since he planned it. Seeing their brother struck down and not knowing who would be next, the other brothers quickly mounted their donkeys and hurriedly left for safety.

Before the brothers arrived home, word came to David that all his sons had been killed (II Samuel 13:29-30). This immediately plunged him into unbearable grief and despair. He tore his clothing and lay on the floor. His servants mourned with him. tearing their clothing. In this dark moment Jonadab stepped forth. Naturally, he somehow managed to have an accurate report. He knew the particulars of this horrible event. It would be interesting to know if he was made aware before or after the murder, but there is no indication in the passage. David's sons, save one, were returning home, he assured David. The one son who was killed was Amnon.

Absalom had fled by this time, knowing his own life was now in danger. David considered raising an army and tracking Absalom down but in the end, did nothing. In fact, he missed his beloved Absalom.

After the murder, Absalom fled to his maternal grandfather in Geshur. It was there he remained for three years. After that time, he began his campaign to return home. David wanted Absalom. With two older sons both dead, Absalom had become the oldest, and David wanted his son near to him. Finally, Absalom was permitted to return. As with Amnon, we find no record of discipline or correction for the deeds committed from David the father.

Slowly, the handsome and ambitious Absalom began to ingratiate himself to the people and undermine his father, the king.

> After this, Absalom prepared a chariot and horses for himself, and fifty men to run before him. Absalom rose up early, and stood beside the way of the gate. When any man had a suit which should come to the king for judgment, then Absalom called to him, and said, "What city are you from?"
>
> He said, "Your servant is of one of the tribes of Israel."
>
> Absalom said to him, "Behold, your matters are good and right; but there is no man deputized by the king to hear you." Absalom said moreover, "Oh that I were made judge in the land, that every man who has any suit or cause might come to me, and I would do him justice!" It was so, that when any man came near to bow down to him, he stretched out his hand, and took hold of him, and kissed him. Absalom did this sort of thing to all Israel who came to the king for judgment. So Absalom stole the hearts of the men of Israel. (II Samuel 15:1-6)

Finally, Absalom makes his move and open insurrection and rebellion breaks out. The heir apparent, shows neither the patience or inclination to wait "his turn." He thought he could take the kingdom. Sadly, he did not factor in God's will and his personal destiny. Power seemed within his grasp. Absalom openly humiliated his father. David fled the city.

This was a bridge too far. There was a counselor who was known for his wisdom, and Absalom sought his advice. The advice reflected what Ahithophel thought would work in his own personal best interest. If Absalom defiled his father's concubine, that would be seen as unforgivable. It would give courage to Absalom's followers as he would be burning the bridge back home. Ahithophel knew that if father and son reconciled, he would never be trusted again. He needed Absalom to win and secure his own position of power.

The women, of course, were of little importance. Their rape and defilement was designed to send a statement to King David. Like Tamar, they were of little human significance. The rape of women has, for centuries, been one of the realities of war. It continues today around the globe. Rape and molestation, in times of war, can be a show of power. It is a message to the men that they cannot even protect their own wives and children, those who are closest to their hearts. It is designed to be a manifestation of the power, virility and authority of the antagonist and the weakness and impotency of their declared enemy. In these situations, rape may be less a sexual offence than a power play that is manifested through sexual behavior.

Tragically Absalom took counsel with Ahithophel and followed his harmful advice.

> Then Absalom said to Ahithophel, "Give your counsel what we shall do." Ahithophel said to Absalom, "Go in to your father's concubines that he has left to keep the house. Then all Israel will

hear that you are abhorred by your father. Then
the hands of all who are with you will be strong."
(II Samuel 16:20–21)

The acts were designed as theater. They were completed
on the top of the house so that all in the city would become
aware of what was going on.

> So they spread a tent for Absalom on the top of
> the house, and Absalom went in to his father's
> concubines in the sight of all Israel. The counsel of
> Ahithophel, which he gave in those days, was as if
> a man inquired at the inner sanctuary of God. All
> the counsel of Ahithophel both was like this with
> David and with Absalom (II Samuel 16:22–23).

Absalom did what Amnon had done to his sister.
Having seen the pain and grief of rape on her face, one would
think he would never do that to a woman, but one would
be mistaken. A tent was set up, and David's concubines
were openly raped for all to see. He had become that which
he clearly hated, that which prompted him to kill his own
brother, an abuser of women. Clearly, this was problematic.
The law condemns this type of action, and even without
the law, respect for one's father would prevent it: "The
nakedness of thy father's wife shalt thou not uncover: it is
thy father's nakedness" (Leviticus 18:8).

The former child of promise was moving in his own
power with the advice of someone who had no investment
in peace and reconciliation. In fact, any resolution

between father and son would work to the detriment of the counselor. The king would not trust him and the son would have no need of him. Ahithophel's advice was self-serving. The women, left to take care of the home when David fled, were clearly victims. They, too, were collateral damage. The cost of sin is spreading, its venom infecting the innocent. Despite all that Absalom did to take power without God on his side, without submitting his life to the Lord, it was futile. He loses the war and his life. In an ironic twist, the beautiful hair that was admired and envied was his undoing.

> Absalom happened to meet David's servants. Absalom was riding on his mule, and the mule went under the thick boughs of a great oak, and his head caught hold of the oak, and he was taken up between the sky and earth; and the mule that was under him went on. A certain man saw it, and told Joab, and said, "Behold, I saw Absalom hanging in an oak." Joab said to the man who told him, "Behold, you saw it, and why didn't you strike him there to the ground? I would have given you ten pieces of silver, and a sash." The man said to Joab, "Though I should receive a thousand pieces of silver in my hand, I still wouldn't stretch out my hand against the king's son; for in our hearing the king commanded you and Abishai and Ittai, saying, 'Beware that no one touch the young man Absalom.' Otherwise if I had dealt falsely against his life (and there is no matter hidden from the king), then you yourself would have set yourself against me."

Then Joab said, "I'm not going to wait like this with you." He took three darts in his hand, and thrust them through the heart of Absalom, while he was yet alive in the middle of the oak. Ten young men who bore Joab's armor surrounded and struck Absalom, and killed him (II Samuel 18:9–15).

When David heard the news of his beloved son's death, he was overcome with grief. He never stopped loving his child even when Absalom was trying to kill him. A third son was now lost. This is an image of a father's love and a father's pain. Absalom, the most handsome man in the land, dead, his three children fatherless. Tamar's protector and brother are gone. Grief and pain flowed freely as the sword continued to cut through hearts and dreams in the House of David.

Tamar,
The Innocent

f
e
's
ar
re
ful
ny

alf-
ing
ave
om.
ces.
t to

d inadvertently sets the stage for the
ortunate bloodshed and sexual abuse that were
ollow. His decision to betray God's command
odgate of lust, sexual extremes, and abuses.
with sin is that once it appears it takes on a
One lie may require additional lies to support
d then having committed to the lie one has
the details of the created reality (which is
eality), if the ruse is to continue. It may be
o acknowledge the truth and experience the
rt of exposure and move forward. A parent
e with their children cannot be guaranteed
parent who fails to closely parent with
ection, and praise may very well guarantee

Without her knowledge, the innocent Tamar was set adrift in a boat with fatal cracks and fissures. She thought she had a future and sadly could only look back on the past and dream of what might have been. Socially, women have long been seen as possessions, trophies, and the means through which men obtain their immortality. Their sons carry their names into the future, and as long as their names are spoken, they continue to be a force in the world, if only in a minor way. During this season, much of a woman's value centered on her youth, reproductive potential, virginity, and pedigree. If her parents were high ranking, she could be married off to a person of wealth and position; if not, the parents were left to negotiate an appropriate match.

Tamar was the daughter of King David, the sister of Absalom, who was the third in line to the throne, then the second, and then the first. Her mother was Maacah, David third wife. daughter of King Talmai of Geshur. Both Tama and Absalom were noted for their good looks; they we striking in appearance. As a princess, she wore a beauti garment, similar in appearance to Joseph's coat of ma colors. She was highly respected.

When Tamar was directed to attend to her h brother, Amnon, it is doubtful that she thought anyth of it. After all, he was her half- brother. She may not h even been worried when he sent everyone out of the ro Apparently, she was totally unprepared for his advan At that moment, she knew she had to persuade him n harm her. Her life, her future, hung in the balance.

Amnon, unwilling to acknowledge the true nature of his drive and feelings, or simply at his young age unable to define the twisted and perverted spirit that was within him, called it love. The dark cloud hanging in the room, the violation felt by his sister, the anger of his father and the hatred that later festered in the heart of Absalom all testify to the fact that love had no place in the room.

> Amnon said to Tamar, "Bring the food into the room, that I may eat from your hand." Tamar took the cakes which she had made, and brought them into the room to Amnon her brother. When she had brought them near to him to eat, he took hold of her, and said to her, "Come, lie with me, my sister!"
>
> She answered him, "No, my brother, do not force me! For no such thing ought to be done in Israel. Don't you do this folly. As for me, where would I carry my shame? And as for you, you will be as one of the fools in Israel. Now therefore, please speak to the king; for he will not withhold me from you."
>
> However he would not listen to her voice; but being stronger than she, he forced her, and lay with her. (2 Samuel 13:10–14)

Tamar negotiated for her life. She appealed to his sense of fairness and justice, respect for the law, when she pointed out that such behavior was condemned in Israel. She reminded him that if he spoke to the king, they could be married. There were alternatives, and she pleaded with him to choose one. The behavior was clearly condemned and the punishment was severe.

> Now Jacob heard that he had defiled Dinah, his daughter; and his sons were with his livestock in the field. Jacob held his peace until they came. Hamor, the father of Shechem went out to Jacob to talk with him. The sons of Jacob came in from the field when they heard it. The men were grieved, and they were very angry, because he had done folly in Israel in lying with Jacob's daughter, a thing that ought not to be done. (Genesis 34:5-7)

It was a noble argument that showed both an awareness of the history and the laws that governed Israel. This would impact someone who was committed to following the law, someone who loved God. In this case, the plea for behavior that God required fell on deaf ears. Tamar suggested that if he, heir apparent to the throne, did such a thing, he would lower himself and be no better than a con artist or ruffian in the street. Surely, no prince would want to be thought of in this manner.

In a subtle, eloquent play on words, Tamar warns Amnon that if he were to do this "outrage [*nevelah*]"—a term associated with the collective shame carried by the violated woman's body (Genesis 34:7, Judges 19:23–24, 20:6, 10)—he would be like one of the "scoundrels [*nevelim*]" in Israel. (Adelman, n.d.)

So close to the fulfillment of his passionate desires, he was not dissuaded. Finally, knowing that her time was running out, Tamar pointed out that if he asked his father, surely, he would give her in marriage to her half-brother. It is unclear that that could happen, but there is reason to believe that he might have been permitted to do so. According to rabbinic tradition (*Sanhedrin 21a*, n.d.), Amnon could have married Tamar as she was conceived prior to her mother's conversion (Encyclopaedia Judaica, n.d.).

To be clear, this point of view is not universal. The problem revolved around the fact that even a single instance of carnal knowledge of a captured beauty is forbidden. Hence, David was compelled to wait until he married Ma'akhah and Tamar, their offspring, was a legitimate child. In this event, Amnon was a half-brother and couldn't consider assaulting his half-sister. Even the school of opinion that argued that a one-time sex encounter was permissible would find it difficult to explain how Tamar could envision a marriage between her and Amnon. After all, he was her half- brother. The Tosafot takes the easy way out of the dilemma by proposing that Ma'akhah was already pregnant with Tamar before David captured her.' Hence, she was not a blood relation of Amnon. In any event, the basic fact remains: that where there is a sanctification, Kiddushin, of a marriage, there exists a brother-sister status between their offspring (Chill, n.d.) .It should be noted that Ma'akhah is the Hebrew form of Maacah. The passage is referring to the same person.

The reality is that if Amnon would consent to talking to David, it would buy time and Tamar could escape immediate danger. She offered all she could, but after listening (or appearing to listen), nothing changed. She tried reason and logic, but they were ineffective in changing his mind. Amnon overpowered her, abused her, taking the valued gift she wanted to share with her future husband. She was now, in the mind of society, ruined, her dreams of a happy life of marriage, children, grandchildren dead. Everything over, everything lost, for Amnon to have a few minutes of pleasure at her expense.

The deed was done, and now when he looked at her, he no longer saw irresistible beauty but absolute repulsion and disgust. Tamar was just a reminder of his lack of control, his inability to be what his father wanted and maybe even what he wanted of himself, to be a man of honor. He has broken her heart and spirit, and he didn't want to see the result of his actions. He wanted to pretend it either didn't happen or it didn't matter. This mass of humanity moaning and crying at his feet had nothing to do with him. He wanted to be rid of it, rid of the memory of it. She needed to be out of his sight, not just now but forever. He called his servant to remove her, and the door was locked behind her. Out of sight, she would be out of mind. He was in line to the throne and deserved whatever he wanted. Sometimes the planning, the desire, and lustful dreams are more rewarding than the reality with someone who had to be forced and attacked.

Some years ago a group of college students were teasing a professor about a young woman who clearly appeared to be flirting with him. The next class meeting, he walked in and wrote on the board, "The imagination is much more interesting than the realistic fact." He turned and gave a quick smile to the group who understood what he meant and went on with the class. It was an off-the-books lesson from the psychology professor. After a while, the students who had teased him understood what he meant. First, he would not touch any of his students inappropriately, and second, an inappropriate response was clearly not worth it since the reality of any inappropriate contact could not measure up to any fantasy he might entertain. The teacher was not about to become guilty of confusing some imagined encounter with the reality of the harm and disappointment the wrong behavior would cause, it wasn't worth it. Unfortunately, this was a lesson Amnon never learned.

Now Amnon was filled with hate and probably no small measure of confusion.

> Then Amnon hated her with exceedingly great hatred; for the hatred with which he hated her was greater than the love with which he had loved her. Amnon said to her, "Arise, be gone!" She said to him, "Not so, because this great wrong in sending me away is worse than the other that you did to me!" But he would not listen to her. Then he called his servant who ministered to him, and said, "Now put this woman out from me, and bolt the door after her." (II Samuel 13:15-17)

Having destroyed Tamar's hopes for the future, after refusing to even talk to King David about the possibility of marriage, like a used tissue, she was discarded. Tragically, it is not a rare feeling.

> She had a garment of various colors on her; for the king's daughters who were virgins dressed in such robes. Then his servant brought her out and bolted the door after her. Tamar put ashes on her head, and tore her garment of various colors that was on her; and she laid her hand on her head, and went her way, crying aloud as she went. (II Samuel 13:18–19).

She was thrown out of her brother's room and sent to reenter the world, a world that would never be the same for her again. She openly wept and mourned. She tore her beautiful royal garments, a teenage girl with a bright future enters the room but a desolate, lonely, shamed woman leaves. Everyone now looked down on her as a ruined woman. These situations were not unheard of, and there was a process that had developed over time. There must be some justice. Witnesses needed to be contacted. Amnon needed to face consequences for his actions. Tamar desperately needed someone, someone to reach out to her.

The one person who came to give her comfort was Absalom. The common reaction to such a violation tends to be the same regardless of cultural setting. Relatives around the world tend to prefer to "keep it as quiet as possible." She would not return to the palace. It was too much to live with, falling from the privileged select group, a princess to just another ruined woman looked down on and pitied. Tamar went to Absalom's house and remained there indefinitely. She was now unfit for marriage except to her rapist, and he had rejected her. It is unclear how long she lived there, but with no further information, she probably spent the rest of her life in the shadows for "her transgressions."

Absalom took the matter to King David, but there is no record that the king ever attempted to comfort his daughter or punish the wrongdoer. Perhaps he too just wanted the whole matter to go away. The bloodletting of the sword sweeping through the House of David is far from finished.

CHAPTER 19

Collateral Damage

Collateral damage is a painful reality in military conflict. Schools filled with children, hospitals with medical professionals and patients, and innocent people just living their lives in their own homes, walking down the street, they have all felt the impact of becoming collateral damage. As unintended targets, they just happened to be in the vicinity and had the course of their lives changed. When an intended target is struck and damage, or death is caused nearby, that damage is collateral. The word comes from the Latin word *collateralis*, which means "together with."

Children are frequently collateral damage in their Parents' divorce. They may find themselves caught in the middle, asked to take sides or spy on one of their parents. They may find that their own lives are upended as they have to move, change schools, try to comfort their parents and hold in their own pain. Children have frequently been collateral damage in violent marriages, trying to keep the peace, trying not to do the wrong thing and make the volatile parent angry. Some homes even make their animals part of the carnage as dogs and cats learn to read the room and hide to avoid being kicked, or screamed at.

The standard MO (Modus Operandi) for sin and evil is indiscriminate destruction. Collateral damage is not so collateral. Evil doesn't care who is destroyed, everyone is fair game. A drunk driver may not intend to hit a child crossing the street, but inhibitions down, reaction time slowed, and double vision operative can bring results that just can't be anticipated.

Nathan told David what to expect, but nothing could prepare him for what his family would experience. David wanted Bathsheba but had no idea of all the people who would be hurt and killed because of his selfish act. David loved God and repented when confronted by the truth. Repentance is necessary.

> Nathan said to David, "You are the man. This is what Yahweh, the God of Israel, says: 'I anointed you king over Israel, and I delivered you out of the hand of Saul. I gave you your master's house, and your master's wives into your bosom, and gave you the house of Israel and of Judah; and if that would have been too little, I would have added to you many more such things. Why have you despised Yahweh's word, to do that which is evil in his sight? You have struck Uriah the Hittite with the sword, and have taken his wife to be your wife, and have slain him with the sword of the

children of Ammon. Now therefore the sword will never depart from your house, because you have despised me, and have taken Uriah the Hittite's wife to be your wife.'

"This is what Yahweh says: 'Behold, I will raise up evil against you out of your own house; and I will take your wives before your eyes, and give them to your neighbor, and he will lie with your wives in the sight of this sun. For you did this secretly, but I will do this thing before all Israel, and before the sun.'"

David said to Nathan, "I have sinned against Yahweh."

Nathan said to David, "Yahweh also has put away your sin. You will not die.(II Samuel 12:7-13).

Sin does not go unpunished. David had tried to cover his tracks and thought he could move on, but there is a consequence for decisions and behaviors. God was gracious. He was kind, and he takes care of his people. David was at the top of his game, which is a dangerous place to be. It is easy to forget who opened the doors, who gave favor. From a high vantage point, sometimes the air gets a little thinner, and it is easy to get light headed. It is easy to think we somehow have earned our way with our talent, skills, and abilities. It's easy to think that we are more powerful than we really are.

Our strength and power come from God, and when we forget or ignore that, problems will come our way. Sin does not plan to stay in a corner of our lives. It spreads like the cancer it is, and it will not be controlled, except by the power of God. The beautiful Tamar had her life destroyed. It was nothing she had done but a consequence of the sins of her father. Even after he found out about the sin of his son, he would not hold Amnon accountable. When Absalom was killed, David openly mourned the loss of his handsome son. He sought God for the life of Bathsheba's child, but what of Tamar? When he was restored to the kingdom, he took care of his concubine who had been raped by Amnon. They were treated as widows, and he was never intimate with them again. We don't know how long Tamar lived, if she remained in her brother's house or if David brought her to his house after Absalom died. David's parenting skills were not as strong as they could have been. In his daughter's hour of greatest pain, he may have chosen not to see her. We can only hope that he came to himself and restored his relationship with his beautiful daughter.

CHAPTER 20

What Is in the Blood?

Compassion and justice are not mutually exclusive. Too often justice is seen as a cruel and heartless reckoning, while compassion is pushed to the side as being weak and useless. It is possible for them to coexist and rightfully so. God demands fairness and justice, and yet he offers compassion. It is difficult and challenging to find the right balance in our lives in any circumstance but especially so when it comes to those we love most, those with whom we share our lives and those whose physical and emotional characteristics so closely reflect our own lives and our hopes for the future.

Children are in many ways, our greatest blessing and our greatest challenge. Our time is so limited to prepare them for the world, and yet we must. God provides us with direction, and even so, we frequently falter when it comes to the matter of compassion, justice, and fairness especially in the family. No one, especially leaders, want to be too hard on their family. No one wants to lose the love and affection of their children. It can be very difficult to hold our loved ones to the same level of accountability as other children we may teach, coach, or serve as scout leaders or Sunday school teachers. In addition, there is the matter of modeling the behavior we want to see in our children. Parenting is no easy task. Matthew Henry rightly points out that

> Grace does not run in the blood, but corruption does. We do not find that David's children imitated him in his devotion; but his false steps they trod in, and in those did much worse, and repented not. Parents know not. How fatal the consequences may be if, in any instance, they give their children bad examples (Henry, n.d.).

Every person falters, but this too can become a tool for teaching young people how to repent, recover, and not be held captive to a poor decision. Parents are not charged to model perfection but how to live a life that has been redeemed by the grace of God. Young people must be shown how to repent. David was honest about his mistakes and repented to God. He was humble. Even so, these are features of his character that his sons chose not to emulate.

The House of David, as many great dynasties, before and after suffered when a son or daughter stepped into power and lacked the former leader's skill and strength of personality. Sometimes a strong leader is followed by an offspring that lacks the necessary spiritual and moral center to lead and in some cases to even appreciate the weight of the office and the necessity of being sensitive to God's leading. Others suffer as well as the leader themselves. The past can be inspirational, informative, and also instructive. The House of David speaks to the world in all of these areas.

Tamar lived her life in extremes. She was the daughter of a well-loved king, and by every report, she was a kind and good person who was respected in her own right. Tamar, within minutes of her encounter with Amnon, saw a change in her status, her world, and her view of herself. There was no gradual letdown—it was simply a collapse of her world. We learn from her life and her pain that no suffering should be pointless or loss. We must learn from what happened to the princess.

The experiences of Tamar are informative. Bad things can happen to good people. We live in an imperfect world, and there will be times and situations over which we have no control that will bring grief and tragedy. The question is not why did these things happen to me, but rather, how will I continue to fulfill my mission and my purpose in spite of the evil that has entered my world.

Some of the most powerful words ever spoken to me came from the lips of a man who had spent weeks in a coma and awoke, partly paralyzed, and yet still found a way to smile and take each day one at a time. He was neither rich nor notable to most people, but every day he pushed himself to accomplish his goals for that day. I met him as he was walking, with some challenges along a damaged sideway. He was coming from the grocery store. He really did need a ride and didn't have one, so he was walking from the bus stop. As I stopped to take him home, he shared with me words that I continue to remember years later. His words to me were "God always sends somebody to help."

I didn't do him a favor that day. He did me a favor. His faith has strengthened me along my way. God does make provisions. As a teenage girl, broken and lost, crying out, walking away from her brother, Amnon, who had destroyed her life, Tamar walked into the brother who helped save her. He rescued her. It was the "wicked Absalom." He gave shelter and comfort to her when she needed it most. He was there for her when her own father did not seem to involve himself with his wounded and frightened daughter. It was Absalom who showed compassion and later named his own daughter Tamar. The older Tamar's future was destroyed, but perhaps through her niece, Tamar, there might still be joy in the future, hope in the future. There was a child who carried her family's blood who would walk into the future, in her stead, hopefully she was as beautiful and intelligent as her dishonored aunt. Tamar brings our attention to another matter which we cannot ignore. She was silenced by society, by her family, but her message still rings out.

What of those who are sexually assaulted? Will we still turn our heads, cry ruined, and punish the innocent for the acts of another? Every day, every sixty-eight seconds, to be exact, someone is sexually assaulted in the United States (Rainn, n.d.). The United States is not alone in the prevalence of sexual assaults. It happens everywhere, and it must be condemned everywhere. It happens to men, women, and children, and it must not be hidden and ignored. Tamar was told to be quiet, but is silence the answer? Families don't want people to know that there is an abuser in their household, and they protect the guilty while leaving the victim to a lifetime of suffering and wondering what they could have done differently. We learn from the beautiful and intelligent Tamar that silencing the victim does not make the problem go away. David's son Amnon might have felt he escaped the punishment for his sin but as happens so often, his affection and alliance with sin provided his own undoing. He did not repent and was destroyed by his own brother. Tamar, as so many others, was not allowed to speak the truth.

Sin may appear to be hidden, but like a cancer not yet detected, all the while, it is quietly destroying a person. By the time the individual is aware, the damage may be extensive. It may be some time before it is acknowledged for what it truly is, not an inconvenience, pain, or discomfort, but a deadly disease intent on destruction. How much better it is to act early and take action against the poisonous tumor. The cancer in the household needed to be treated. Hiding sin in the camp didn't work for the House of David, and it will not work for us.

The past can be instructive. Someone must speak for the ones who have been silenced. We must both acknowledge the poisonous nature of sin and seek God for forgiveness and restoration. There would be collateral damage for David's sin just as original sin has left its mark.

The prophet spoke. The sword had to come, but it did not have to linger except for the refusal to repent.

Amnon had a window of two years before the sharp edge of the sword glided through the air destroying his life. Amnon could have repented, offered to marry Tamar, humbled himself before God and man, but instead, he made a conscious decision to "stick to his guns." It is highly probable that Amnon was that child and young adult who could do no wrong. He had great potential but needed direction and discipline. Consequences may be delayed but not suspended forever.

Amnon sadly lost his life when, had he chosen to repent, to accept responsibility, it might have been spared. It is certain that Amnon would have been punished, but perhaps he could have lived out his days redeemed. We do not know because he did not make that choice. We do know that God hears the sincere cry of the heart. His ear was attentive, but there is no record of regret or repentance on the part of Amnon.

Tamar is gone, but every day there are thousands who need someone to stand in the gap and provide protection, shelter, understanding, and an arm around the shoulder. Every day a victim needs a parent, a family member, a church member, a teacher, or preacher to open their eyes and see what they do not want to see, to offer shelter and protection to those who need it most. There is much to condemn in the ambitious rebellious Absalom, but in this one thing, perhaps we should emulate him. We should not turn our heads but offer comfort to those who have been neglected, abused, and abandoned in our families and in our societies. We must stand and speak for those who cannot speak for themselves. We must be advocates for the Tamars who remain.

Sin is no solo event. There are people all around us who are impacted by our behaviors and actions. We can create a blessed atmosphere for those who are around us or create a battlefield littered with damaged and hurting people. We do not live our lives in isolation. We live in a community. It is that very fact that becomes so important in living a life that influences people for good and touches others in such a way that their lives are better because of us. Neither sin nor holiness exists in a vacuum. Will our lives result in a sword that will cut through generations with sadness and havoc, or will it create a climate where people will be challenged to consider the claims of Jesus Christ, where others can see the gospel lived out loud and know that living for God is not a myth but a very real and blessed reality?

May we all live our lives to glorify God and to leave a heritage of holiness.

WORKS CITED

Accounting for the Prophets. (n.d.). Ohr Somayach. Retrieved February 10, 2022, from https://ohr.edu/ask_db/ask_main.php/220/Q3/.

Adelman , R. Last updated June 23. (n.d.). *Tamar 2*. Jewish Women's Archive. Retrieved April 2, 2022, from https://jwa.org/encyclopedia/article/tamar-27.

Balsamo, M. (2021, April 15). *Ponzi schemer Bernie Madoff dies in prison at 82*. AP NEWS. Retrieved February 6, 2022, from https://apnews.com/article/bernie-madoff-dead-9d9b d8065708384e0bf0c840bd1ae711.

CBS Interactive. (2021, August 24). *NYPD: Woman raped in rideshare car on Staten Island*. CBS News. Retrieved April 1, 2022, from https://www.cbsnews.com/newyork/news/nypd-woman-raped-in-rideshare-car-on-staten-island/.

Chill, A. (n.d.). The Sidrot Insights into the Weekly Torah Reading. Google Books. Retrieved

April 2, 2022, from https://books.google. /
books?id=R4kRjk21FLkC&pg=PA14&lpg=
P14&dq=could% 2Btamar%2
Blegally%2Bmarry%2Bamnon&source=
bl&ots=N_cUmJMk0U&sig=ACfU3U3b_WwO-
IWy1LPl5k8BLb5fg-GNdA&hl=en&sa=X&ved=
2ahUKEwjK4oTBofb2AhXGKs 0KHXH2D
wkQ6AF6BAhBEAM #v=onepage&q=could%20
tamar%20legally%20marry%20amnon&f=false.

Coffman, J. B. (n.d.). *Coffman's Commentaries on
the Bible-The Sword Comes to David's House.*
StudyLight.org. Retrieved March 28, 2022, from
https://www.studylight.org/commentaries/
eng/bcc/2-samuel-13.html#verse-1.

De-Whyte, J. P. (2018). *Wom(b)an: A cultural-
narrative reading of the Hebrew BibleBarrenness
narratives* (Vol. 162, Ser. Biblical Interpretation
Series). Brill. Retrieved February 24, 2022,
from https://brill.com/view/title/33599.

DeYoung, K. (1987, August 11). *The making of a marriage.*
The Washington Post. Retrieved February 11, 2022,
from https://www.washingtonpost.com/ archive/
lifestyle/1987/08/11/ the-making-of-a-marriage/
cc7f1946-176e-4e00-94ae-1402c7eb7640/.

Driscoll, P. M. (2005, August 12). *Convict finds salvation in
prison cell, becomes pastor and counselor.* The Seattle
Times. Retrieved February 6, 2022, from https://

www.seattletimes.com/news/convict-finds-salvation-in-prison-cell-becomes-pastor-and-counselor/.

Encyclopaedia Judaica. (n.d.). Amnon. Retrieved April 2, 2022, from https://www.jewishvirtuallibrary.org/amnon.

13 Facts about Leah Everyone Should Know - Jewish History. https://www.chabad.org/library/article_cdo/aid/4943195/jewish/13-Facts-About-Leah-Everyone-Should-Know.htm.

Farber, Z. (2017). *How Is It Possible that Jacob Mistakes Leah for Rachel?* thetorah.com.retrieved February 12, 2022, from https://www.thetorah.com/article/how-is-it-possible-that-jacob-mistakes-leah-for-rachel*10 fun facts about sheep*. BC SPCA. (2022, March 21). Retrieved October 16, 2022, from https://spca.bc.ca/news/fun-facts-about-sheep/.

Fairchild, M. (2020, June 15). *Learn how absalom's rebellion caused a violent downfall.* Learn Religions. Retrieved April 1, 2022, from https://www.learnreligions.com/absalom-facts-4138309

Golding, N. (n.d.). *Cave of the patriarchs (me'arat hamachpelah) - chabad.org.* Cave of the Patriarchs (Me'arat Hamachpelah). Retrieved February 14, 2022, from https://www.chabad.org/library/article_cdo/aid/588225/jewish/Cave-of-the-Patriarchs-Mearat-Hamachpelah.htm.

Henriksen Garroway, kristine. (n.d.). *Bride-price: The Story of Jacob's Marriage to Rachel and Leah*. Bride-Price: The Story of Jacob's Marriage to Rachel and Leah - TheTorah.com. Retrieved October 15, 2022, from https://www.thetorah.com/article/bride-price-the-story-of-jacobs-marriage-to-rachel-and-leah.

Henry, M. (n.d.). *Matthew Henry's Commentary on the Whole Bible*. 2 Samuel 13 Matthew Henry's commentary on the whole Bible. Retrieved April 12, 2022, from

https://biblehub.com/commentaries/mhcw/2_samuel/13.htm.

Hersch, E. G., & Seligsohn, M. (Eds.). (1906). *Jewishencyclopedia.com*. RACHEL - JewishEncyclopedia.com. Retrieved February 7, 2022, from https://jewishencyclopedia.com/articles/12521-rachel.

Hindustan Times. (2021, November 25). *Young woman raped in moving car, accused arrested*.

Hindustan Times. Retrieved April 1, 2022, from https://www.hindustantimes.com/cities/lucknow-news/young-woman-raped-in-moving-car-accused-arrested-101637862030764.html.

IMDb.com. (n.d.). *Benazir Bhutto*. IMDb. Retrieved February 11, 2022, from https://m.imdb.com/name/nm1567097/quotes.

Jewishencyclopedia.com. RACHEL - JewishEncyclopedia.com. (n.d.). Retrieved February 7, 2022, from https://

jewishencyclopedia.com/articles/12521-rachel Kadari, T. (n.d.). *Leah: Midrash and aggadah*. Jewish Women's Archive. Retrieved February 9, 2022, from https://jwa. org/encyclopedia/article/leah-midrash-and-aggadah.

Kadari, T. (n.d.). *Leah: Midrash and aggadah*. Jewish Women's Archive. Retrieved February 9, 2022, from https://jwa.org/encyclopedia/ article/leah-midrash-and-aggadah.

King David (c.1040 - c.970 BCE). King David. (n.d.). Retrieved March 23, 2022, from https://www. jewishvirtuallibrary.org/king-david.

Knox, J. S. (2022, March 24). *King David*. World History Encyclopedia. Retrieved March 25, 2022, from https://www.worldhistory.org/King_David/.

Laban - Jewish history - chabad.org. (n.d.). Retrieved February 22, 2022, from https://www.chabad.org/ library/article_cdo/aid/3179/jewish/Laban.htm Marriage and Betrothal in Bible Times. Lion tracks QNA—how did marriage and betrothal work in Bible times? (n.d.). Retrieved October 15, 2022, from https://www.bibleistrue.com/qna/qna22.htm.

Marriage and Betrothal in Bible Times. Lion tracks QNA— how did marriage and betrothal work in Bible times? (n.d.). Retrieved October 15, 2022, from https://www.bibleistrue.com/qna/qna22.htm.

Mindel, N. (n.d.). *Eli the high priest - 2772 - 10 iyar 2870/2871 - jewish ..* Eli,the High Priest. Retrieved April 1, 2022, from https://www.chabad.org/library/article_cdo/aid/112391/jewish/Eli-The-High-Priest.htm.

Moss, A. (n.d.). *Who is Adina? - biblical women - chabad.org*. TheJewishWoman.org. Retrieved February 22, 2022, from https://www.chabad.org/theJewishWoman/article_ cdo/aid/ 4675456/jewish/Who-Is-Adina.htm.

New Boston Church of Christ. (2014, December 12). *Sin and its characteristics - new Boston Church of Christ.* https://newbostoncoc.org/kevins-korner/sin-and-its-characteristics/. Retrieved March 21, 2022, from https://newbostoncoc.org/kevins-korner/sin-and-its-characteristics/.

Sanhedrin 21a. (n.d.). Sanhedrin 21a. Retrieved January 6, 2023, from https://www.sefaria.org/Sanhedrin.21a?lang=bi

Sin – Encyclopedia Volume – Catholic Encyclopedia. Catholic Online. (n.d.). Retrieved March 20, 2022, from https://www.catholic.org/encyclopedia/view.php?id=10849.

Singer, I., and Lauterbach, J. Z. (n.d.). *Jewishencyclopedia. com.* TAMAR . Retrieved April 2, 2022, from https://www.jewishencyclopedia.com/articles/14222-tamar.

Staff, B. A. S. (2022, June 15). *The Tel Dan Inscription: The first historical evidence of king david from the Bible.* Biblical Archaeology Society. Retrieved October 17, 2022, from https://www.biblicalarchaeology.org/daily/

biblical-artifacts/the-tel-dan-inscription-the-first-historical-evidence-of-the-king-david-bible-story/.

The disturbing story of David's ten concubines. Marg Mowczko. (2021, August 25). Retrieved April 2, 2022, from https://margmowczko.com/davids-ten-concubines/.

Tzvi. "Women in the Bible #3: Rachel & Leah Part 1 - Aish.com Women in the Bible, the Bible, Judaism 101." *Aish.com*, 19 Dec. 2021, https://aish.com/women-in-the-bible-rachel-leah-part-1/.

Victims of sexual violence: Statistics. RAINN. (n.d.). Retrieved April 4, 2022, from https://www.rainn.org/statistics/victims-sexual-violence.

World English Bible (WEB) - Version Information - BibleGateway.com. (n.d.). Retrieved October 25, 2022, from https://www.biblegateway.com/versions/World-English-Bible-WEB/

Young woman raped in moving car, accused arrested. Hindustan Times. (2021, November 25). Retrieved April 1, 2022, from https://www.hindustantimes.com/cities/lucknow-news/young-woman-raped-in-moving-car-accused-arrested-101637862030764.html.